Patience
with
God

Patience

with

God

جو

THE STORY OF ZACCHAEUS
CONTINUING IN US

جو

Tomáš Halík

Translated from Czech into English by Gerald Turner

DOUBLEDAY

New York   London   Toronto   Sydney   Auckland

DD

DOUBLEDAY

Copyright © 2009 by Tomáš Halík

All Rights Reserved

Published in the United States by Doubleday,
an imprint of The Crown Publishing Group,
a division of Random House, Inc., New York.
www.doubleday.com

DOUBLEDAY and the DD colophon are registered trademarks of
Random House, Inc.

Book design by Donna Sinisgalli

Library of Congress Cataloging-in-Publication Data
Halík, Tomáš.
Patience with God : the story of Zacchaeus continuing in us / by
Tomáš Halík. — 1st ed.
p. cm.
Includes bibliographical references.
1. Zacchaeus (Biblical figure) 2. Patience—Religious aspects—
Christianity. 3. Trust in God. I. Title.
BS2520.Z3H35 2009
242'.5—dc22
2008036475

ISBN 978-0-385-52449-0

PRINTED IN THE UNITED STATES OF AMERICA

3 5 7 9 10 8 6 4 2

First Edition

The prophet refers to some men saying: When they say to you: You are not our brothers, you are to tell them: You are our brothers. Consider whom he intended by these words.

—*St. Augustine*

Patience with others is Love, Patience with self is Hope, Patience with God is Faith.

—*Adel Bestavros*

For the love of God I accept even the strangest thoughts.

—*St. Thérèse de Lisieux*

One of the most exquisite pleasures of human love—to serve the loved one without his knowing it—is only possible, as regards the love of God, through atheism.

—*Simone Weil*

Contents

Introduction

I agree with atheists on many things, often on almost everything—
except their belief that God doesn't exist.

In today's bustling marketplace of religious wares of every kind,
I sometimes feel closer with my Christian faith to the skeptics or to
the atheist or agnostic critics of religion. With certain kinds of atheists I share a sense of God's absence from the world. However, I regard their interpretation of this feeling as too hasty, as an expression
of impatience. I am also often oppressed by God's silence and the
sense of God's remoteness. I realize that the ambivalent nature of the
world and life's many paradoxes can give rise to phrases such as
"God is dead" to explain God's hiddenness. But I can also find other
possible interpretations of the same experience and another possible
attitude to "the absent God." I know of three (mutually and profoundly interconnected) forms of patience for confronting the absence of God. They are called *faith, hope,* and *love.*

Yes, patience is what I consider to be the main difference between faith and atheism. What atheism, religious fundamentalism,
and the enthusiasm of a too-facile faith have in common is how
quickly they can ride roughshod over the mystery we call God—

and that is why I find all three approaches equally unacceptable. One must never consider mystery "over and done with." Mystery, unlike a mere dilemma, cannot be overcome; one must wait patiently at its threshold and persevere in it—must carry it in one's heart—just as Jesus's mother did according to the Gospel, and allow it to mature there and lead one in turn to maturity.

I too could not have been brought to faith by the "proofs of God's existence" found in many pious tomes. If the signs of God's presence lay within easy reach on the surface of the world, as some religious zealots like to think, there would be no need for real faith. Yes, there is also a type of faith that springs from simple joy and enchantment with the world and the way it is—a faith that can be suspected of naïveté, but whose sincerity and authenticity cannot be denied. Faith of this bright and cheerful variety often accompanies the initial "enchantment" of new converts or suddenly shines forth unexpectedly at precious moments on life's journey, sometimes even in the depths of pain. Maybe it is a "foretaste" of the enviable freedom found at the supreme phase of our spiritual journey, the moment of the final and total affirmation of life and the world. It is this affirmation that we sometimes hear described as *"via unitiva"* or *"amor fati,"* as the soul's mystical union with God, or as an understanding and joyful approbation of one's own fate in the sense of Nietzsche's Zarathustra: "Was THAT—life? . . . Well! Once more!"

But I'm convinced that maturing in one's faith also entails accepting and enduring moments—and sometimes even lengthy periods—when God seems remote or remains concealed. What is obvious and demonstrable doesn't require faith. We don't need faith when confronted with unshakable certainties accessible to our powers of reason, imagination, or sensory experience. We need faith precisely at those twilight moments when our lives and the world are full of uncertainty, during the cold night of God's silence. And its function is not to allay our thirst for certainty and safety, but *to teach us to live with mystery.* Faith and hope are expressions of our patience at just such moments—and so is love. Love without patience is not real love. I would say it applies both to "carnal love" and to "love for God," were I not sure that there is in fact only one love, that by its nature it is one, undivided and indivisible. Faith—like love—is inseparably linked to trust and fidelity. And trust and fidelity are proven by patience.

Faith, hope, and love are three aspects of our patience with God; they are three ways of coming to terms with the experience of God's hiddenness. They therefore offer a distinctly different path from either atheism or "facile belief." In contrast with those two frequently proposed shortcuts, however, their path is a long one indeed. It is a path, like the Exodus of the Israelites, that traverses wastelands and darkness. And yes, occasionally the path is also lost; it is a pilgrimage that involves constant searching and losing one's way from time to time. Sometimes we must descend into the deepest abyss and the vale of shadows in order to find the path once more. But if it did not lead there it would not be the path to God; God does not dwell on the surface.

Traditional theology maintained that, simply by contemplating the creation of the world, human reason could be convinced of God's existence—and this is an assertion with which one can still, of course, agree. (Or, more precisely, reason is capable of reaching that conclusion; nevertheless, the world is an ambivalent reality that theoretically admits other perspectives—and just because human reason "is capable" of something, that does not mean that each individual's reason must use that capacity.) Yet traditional theology proclaimed that the human conviction about God's existence was something other than simply faith. Human conviction lies in the realm of "nature," while faith transcends that realm: it is a gift—"infused divine grace." According to Thomas Aquinas, faith is a gift of grace that is infused into human reason, enabling reason to transcend its natural capacity and in a certain limited way to participate in perfect cognition, whereby God recognizes Himself. Yet there remains a tremendous difference between the cognition enabled by faith and the knowledge of God face to face as a "beatific vision" (*visio beatifica*), which is reserved for the saints in heaven (i.e., for us too, if we display the patience of our pilgrim faith and our never-entirely-satisfied longing right up to the threshold of eternity).

If our relationship with God were based solely on a conviction of His existence, which can be acquired painlessly through an emotional appreciation of the world's harmony or a rational computation of a universal chain of causes and effects, it would not be what I have in mind when I speak about faith. According to the ancient teachers of the church, faith is a ray of light whereby God Himself penetrates the dark spaces of human life. God Himself is within it like the touch of His ray of light, in the same way that from an enormous distance the sun touches the earth and our bodies with its warmth. And, of course, as with the sun, there are also moments of eclipse in our relationship with God.

It is hard to decide whether there have been more moments of eclipse in our particular era than there were in the past, or whether we are now more informed about and sensitive to them. It is equally difficult to decide whether the dark mental states of anxiety and grief that so many people undergo in our modern civilization and that we describe in terms taken from clinical medicine—which, in turn, studies them with its resources and from its own standpoint in an effort to eliminate them—are more abundant now than in the past, or whether previous generations paid less attention to them because of other worries, or maybe had other—possibly more effective—ways of treating or confronting them.

These moments of darkness, chaos, and absurdity, of falling from the safety of a rational order, are strikingly reminiscent of what Nietzsche prophesied through the lips of his "madman" who brought the news of the death of God: "How could we drink up the sea? Who gave us the sponge to wipe away the entire horizon? What were we doing when we unchained this earth from its sun? Whither are we moving? Away from all suns . . ."

Such moments of being "far away from all suns," which, on the great historical stage, we label with such symbols as "Auschwitz," "the Gulag," "Hiroshima," "9/11," or "the civilization of death," and at the everyday level of individual lives with the words "depression" or "breakdown," are for many people "the rock of atheism." They are the reason for the conviction that—in the words of Shakespeare's Macbeth—"life is a story told by an idiot . . . signifying nothing," and chaos and absurdity are its be-all and end-all. But there are also people—and the author of this book is one of them—for whom the experience of God's silence and God's hiddenness in this world is the starting point and one of the basic factors of faith itself.

Hardly anything points toward God and calls as urgently for God as the experience of His absence. This experience is capable of leading some to "indict God" and eventually reject faith. There exist, however, particularly in the mystical tradition, many other interpretations of that absence, and other ways of coming to terms with it. Without the painful experience of a "world without God," it is hard for us to grasp the meaning of religious seeking, as well as everything we want to say about "patience with God" and its three aspects—faith, hope, and love.

I'm convinced that a mature faith must incorporate those experiences that some call "the death of God" or—less dramatically—God's silence, although it is necessary to subject such experiences to inner reflection, and also undergo and overcome them honestly, not in a superficial or facile manner. I am not saying to atheists that they are wrong, but that they lack patience. I am saying to them that their truth is an incomplete truth.

Hans Urs von Balthasar liked to use the expression "looting the Egyptians" to describe the Christians' task of adopting the best of "pagan culture," in the way that the Israelites, on their journey out of Egypt, deprived the Egyptians of their gold and silver. Yes, I must admit that when the old atheism of European modernity has passed into oblivion I would regret it if Christianity had not extracted and retained what it contained of "gold," i.e., what was sincere and truthful—even it was the incomplete truth.[1]

But it is necessary to add right away that "our truth," the religious truth of faith here on earth, is in a sense "incomplete" also, because by its intrinsic nature it is an openness toward mystery, which will not be revealed in entirety until the end of time. That is why we must resist the lure of haughty triumphalism. That is why we have something to say to "unbelievers" and those of other faiths. That is why we have to listen and learn. It would be a reprehensible neglect if Christianity failed to use for its own benefit the fact that, during the modern era, it was subject, more than any other religion, to the purgative flames of atheist criticism; it would be just as unfortunate to lack the courage to enter that smelting furnace as to renounce, in the midst of the flames, the faith and hope that are intended to be tested and refined. In the spirit of Paul the apostle, we should not ask for the body of Christianity to be freed from the thorn of atheism. That thorn should instead constantly awaken our faith from the complacency of false certainties, so that we rely more on the power of grace—a grace that shows itself most in our times of weakness.[2]

Atheism can also help "prepare the way of the Lord": it can help us rid our faith of "religious illusions." We mustn't let it have the last word, however, as so many impatient people do. Even at moments of great exhaustion, we should remain receptive to the message like the one brought by the angel to Elijah on his journey to Mount Horeb: Get up and eat, else the journey will be too long for you!

သာ

It would be hard to find two places on the globe that are so utterly disparate as the place where the idea for this book arose and the location where the manuscript was finally written. Like the five books that preceded it, I wrote this almost entirely during my summer vacation in the deep silence and total isolation of a forest hermitage near a monastery in the Rhineland. The idea for it, however, originated during a freezing winter afternoon on one of the most bustling streets of the planet—Broadway in New York—on one of the highest floors of a skyscraper belonging to the Bertelsmann-Doubleday publishing house, in a room with a fascinating view of the snow-covered roofs of Manhattan.

While I was discussing a contract for an English-language version of *Confessor's Night,* publisher Bill Berry was taken by the title of another of my books: the sermon collection *Addressing Zacchaeus.* And when I explained to him why I had used the story of Zacchaeus as a motto for the book, he urged me to develop the "Zacchaeus theme" in a separate book, rather in the way Henri J. M. Nouwen did when he developed his well-known work, *The Return of the Prodigal Son.*

I asked for several days to think it over and spent that time wandering through bustling boulevards of Manhattan. And then, on Fifth Avenue, I stepped into St. Patrick's Cathedral—that sanctum of silence in the vigorously beating heart of the American metropolis—and decided to take up the challenge.

I'd like to thank Bill Berry and my literary agent, Marly Rusoff, once more for their inspirational conversation that day, as well as the fathers of the monastery in the Rhine valley for their kind and discreet hospitality, and all my friends and companions for the prayers that accompanied me during those weeks of meditation and work. Sincere thanks go to my friend Gerry Turner for his efforts with the translation and the difficult task of rendering all the colors, scents, and melodies of the Czech language into the mother tongue of Shakespeare and Cardinal Newman (and in its American guise, moreover).

ᴣ The Gospel Story of Zacchaeus

*He came to Jericho and intended to pass through
the town. Now a man there named Zacchaeus, who
was a chief tax collector and also a wealthy man,
was seeking to see who Jesus was; but he could not
see Him because of the crowd, for he was short in
stature. So he ran ahead and climbed a sycamore
tree in order to see Jesus, who was about to pass
that way. When He reached the place, Jesus looked
up and said to him, "Zacchaeus, come down
quickly, for today I must stay at your house." And
he came down quickly and received Him with joy.
When they all saw this, they began to grumble,
saying, "He has gone to stay at the house of a
sinner." But Zacchaeus stood there and said to the
Lord, "Behold, half of my possessions, Lord, I shall
give to the poor, and if I have extorted anything
from anyone I shall repay it four times over." And
Jesus said to him, "Today salvation has come to this
house because this man too is a descendant of
Abraham. For the Son of man has come to seek and
to save what was lost." ᴣ*

LUKE 19:1–10

Patience

with

God

CHAPTER 1

و

Addressing Zacchaeus

It was early morning and fresh snow lay in the streets of Prague. Everything was fairly fresh in those days—the mid-1990s. A few years earlier, the Communist regime had fallen in the course of the "Velvet Revolution," along with its monopoly of political and police power, and for the first time in decades genuine parliamentary democracy was restored. The church and the university once more enjoyed freedom. That turn of events wrought enormous changes in my life: during the 1970s, I had been secretly ordained abroad at a time of religious repression at home that had already lasted decades. Not even my mother, with whom I lived, was allowed to know I was a priest. For eleven years, I performed my priestly duties clandestinely in an "underground church." Now I was able to function openly, freely, as a priest, without any risk of repression, in the newly created university parish in the heart of Old Prague. After years during which I had to give lectures on philosophy solely as part of clandestine courses in private homes organized by the "flying university," could only publish in samizdat, I was able to return to the university, write for the newspapers, and publish books.

But on that particular winter morning I was headed, not for the church or the university, but for the parliament building. Among the novelties of those days was the custom, established a few years earlier, of inviting a member of the clergy to the parliament once a year, just before Christmas, to deliver a brief meditation to the assembled members of parliament and senators prior to the last sitting before the Christmas vacation.

Yes, everything was still fairly fresh and retained a whiff of newly won freedom. Yet a few years had passed since the "Velvet Revolution," and the first waves of euphoria and its heady confrontation with open spaces were things of the past. The initial illusions had evaporated, and many previously unsuspected problems and complications were appearing in public life. Gradually, something that psychiatrists call "agoraphobia" was creeping into society: a dread of open spaces, literally a fear of the marketplace. Almost everything imaginable was suddenly available on the market in goods and ideas—but many people were confused and puzzled by the enormous diversity of what was on offer and the necessity of making choices. Some of them got a headache from the sudden, blinding profusion of color, and now and then they even began to miss the black-and-white world of yesteryear—although in fact it had been tediously and boringly gray.

I concluded my words to the members of parliament and senators—most of whom had probably never held a Bible in their hands—with a reference to the scene from Luke's Gospel in which Jesus moves through the crowds in Jericho and unexpectedly addresses a chief tax collector who is secretly observing him from the branches of a fig tree.[1]

I compared the story with the behavior of Christians in our country. When, after the fall of Communism, Christ's followers came out freely into the open after so many years, they noticed many people who applauded them and maybe a few who had previously shaken their fists at them. What they didn't notice, however, was *that the trees all around them were full of Zacchaeuses*—those who were unwilling or unable to join the throng of old or brand-new believers, but were neither indifferent nor hostile to them. Those Zacchaeuses were curious seekers, but at the same time they wanted to maintain a certain *distance.* That odd combination of inquisitiveness and expectation, interest and shyness, and sometimes, maybe, even a feeling of guilt and "inadequacy," kept them hidden in their fig trees.

By addressing Zacchaeus *by name,* Jesus emboldened him to come down from his hiding place. He surprised him by wanting to stay in his house even though He risked immediate slander and criticism: "He's accepted the hospitality of a sinner!"

There is no written account of Zacchaeus's ever having joined Jesus's disciples, nor of his having followed Jesus on His travels like the chosen twelve or the throng of other men and women. What we do know, however, is that he decided to change his life, *and salvation came to his house.* In our times, the church has been incapable of addressing its Zacchaeuses in like manner.

I warned the politicians against something similar happening at the civic and political levels. While it was true that many people were still observing the new beginning of democracy in our country—maybe after a certain period of initial general euphoria—with curiosity and some eagerness, for various reasons they also had misgivings and a certain diffidence. But maybe many of them were subconsciously waiting for the moment when they would be addressed or invited directly by someone or something. How many politicians, who spent their time organizing their supporters and contending with opponents, were prepared to understand those *Zacchaeuses,* to take a sincere and respectful interest in them and "address them by name," talk to them, make their acquaintance? Maybe on account of that failure, many "tax collectors" didn't change their lives, many wrongs were not righted, and many hopes were dashed.

Zacchaeus may appear to some to be an incorrigible individualist, an "outsider"; where people are only too ready to line up in enthusiastic or angry ranks, he instinctively seeks a hiding place in the branches of a fig tree. He doesn't do so out of pride, as it might appear; after all, he is well aware of his "small stature" and his great failings, of his shortcomings vis-à-vis absolute postulates and challenges. Yet he is able and willing to abandon his privacy and his detachment if "addressed by name"—then, all of a sudden, he just might accept those absolute challenges and change his life. The only person capable of addressing Zacchaeus, however, is someone for whom those people hidden in the branches of a fig tree are not strangers or aliens—someone who doesn't disdain them, who has concern for them, someone who can respond to what happens in their hearts and minds.

There are plenty of Zacchaeuses in our midst. The fate of our world, our church, and society depends more than we are willing to admit on the extent to which these Zacchaeuses will be won over or not.

ॐ

I finished my meditation, but the story of Zacchaeus was still on my mind. I walked here and there through pre-Christmas Prague and strove to identify why it was that this particular passage had caught my imagination so strongly. And then I realized that this very story could help to achieve a clearer and deeper understanding of what I had long regarded subconsciously as my own particular mission and vocation.

In my pastoral work as a priest, but also in all my other fields of activity—my books and articles, university teaching, and the media—my aim has always been neither "converting the converted," nor caring for the orderly sheep of the flock, nor even engaging in never-ending polemics and disputes with opponents. I don't think my chief vocation ought to be "mission" in the classical sense, if by that one means winning over as many people as possible to one's own church flock or political persuasion. I feel that my chief purpose is to be an understanding neighbor for those who find it impossible to join the exultant crowds beneath the unfurled flags of whatever color, for those *who keep their distance.*

I like Zacchaeuses. I think I have been given the gift of understanding them. People often construe the distance that Zacchaeuses maintain as an expression of their "superiority," but I don't think they are right—things aren't that simple. In my experience, it is more the result of shyness. In some cases, the reason for their aversion to crowds, particularly ones with slogans and banners, is that they suspect that the truth is too fragile to be chanted on the street.

Most of those people did not choose their place "on the margins" voluntarily. It could well be that some of them are also reticent because—like Zacchaeus—they are all too aware that their own house is not in order, and they realize, or at least suspect, that changes need to be made in their own lives. Maybe, unlike the unfortunate person in one of Jesus's parables, they realize they are not properly attired for the wedding and therefore cannot take a seat among the guests of honor at the wedding feast.[2] They are still on the journey, dusty and far from the goal. They are not yet "ready" to display themselves to others in the full light of day, maybe because they find themselves in a blind alley on their life's journey.

And yet they sense the urgent moment when something of importance passes by them. It has a force of attraction, as it had for Zacchaeus, who longed to set eyes on Jesus. But sometimes, as in Zacchaeus's case, they hide their spiritual yearning with fig leaves—from others and sometimes from themselves too.

꒜

The only person capable of addressing Zacchaeus is someone who "knows his name" and knows his secret. Someone for whom this human type is not alien, who is capable of empathizing with the complex reasons for his reticence. *It would seem that the only person truly capable of empathizing with the Zacchaeuses of our days is someone who once was, and to a certain extent still is, a Zacchaeus.* People who feel most at home within the exultant crowds will probably find it hard to understand such a type.

I once saw on the wall of a Prague subway station the inscription "Jesus is the answer," probably written by someone on the way back from some high-spirited evangelistic gathering. Yet someone else had aptly added the words: "But what was the question?" It reminded me of the comment made by the philosopher Eric Voegelin that the biggest problem for today's Christians wasn't that they didn't have the right answers, but that they'd forgotten the question to which they were the answers.

Answers without questions—without the questions that origi-
nally provoked them, but also without the subsequent questions that
are provoked by every answer—are like trees without roots. But
how often are "Christian truths" presented to us like felled, lifeless
trees in which birds can no longer find a nest? (As a young professor, Joseph Ratzinger apparently commented, apropos of Jesus's
parable about the kingdom of heaven being like a tree in which
birds make their nests, that the church is beginning dangerously to
resemble a tree with many dead branches on which there frequently
sit some rather odd birds—although I'm not sure how willing he
would be these days to sign that statement with the pontifical pen
or append the "the fisherman's seal.")

It takes the confrontation of questions and answers to return a
real meaning and dynamic to our statements. Truth *happens* in the
course of dialogue. There is always a temptation to allow our answers to bring to an end the process of searching, as if the topic of
the conversation was a *problem* that has now been solved. But when
a fresh question arrives, the unexhausted depths of *mystery* show
through once more. Let it be said over and over again: faith is not a
question of problems but of *mystery,* so we must never abandon the
path of seeking and asking. Yes, in seeking Zacchaeus we must often shift from problems to mystery, from apparently final answers
back to infinite questions.

ॐ

Paul, the "thirteenth apostle," who did the most to spread the
Gospel, wrote: *I have become all things to all.* Maybe at this time we
will discover Christ's closeness most effectively if we, his disciples,

make ourselves *seekers with those who seek* and *questioners with those who question.* There are more than enough of those who declare they have already reached their goal and offer ready-made but often facile answers, and unfortunately they are also to be found among those who invoke the name of Jesus. Maybe we will make our belief more accessible to the Zacchaeuses of our day if we make them our *neighbors,* in Jesus's sense, as they "look out through the leaves."

I once came across a book by a bishop with the subtitle "a book for seekers and doubters." Out of curiosity I picked it up, particularly as I was personally acquainted with the author and liked him. However, after a few pages, I realized that the subtitle—whether it was the work of the author or of an enterprising publisher—was simply an advertising gimmick. It was evident from the entire tone of the book that the author's attitude to seekers was one of someone who had already found what he wanted, while he regarded doubters as people whose doubts he could easily turn into certainties.

At that moment I decided I would write books of a different kind—as a doubter among doubters and a seeker among seekers. And I soon had the feeling that the Lord had really accepted that intention and taken it even more seriously than I had when the idea first struck me. But in order to ensure that this work would not be a sham, God managed to undermine many of the religious certainties I had previously embraced. In doing so, He prepared at the same time a surprising and very valuable gift for me: at the very moment of "rift," at that moment of shaken and collapsing certainties, at the very moment of more and more questions and doubts, he showed me his face more clearly than ever before.

I realized that the "encounter with God"—conversion, assenting in faith with how God reveals Himself and the church presents that revelation—was not the end of the journey. To have faith means to "follow in the footsteps"; in this world it takes the form of a never-ending journey. True religious faith on earth can never end like a successful search for some object or other—i.e., by finding and possessing—because it is not directed toward some material end, but to the heart of mystery, which is inexhaustible and bottomless.

The path to the Zacchaeuses of today—people often on the fringe or beyond the visible frontiers of the churches, in the zone of questions and doubts, in that singular region between the two fortified camps of those "whose minds are made up" (i.e., self-assured believers and self-assured atheists)—helped me get a fresh understanding of faith and of the One to whom faith relates.

ॐ

Insofar as we are disciples of Christ, we want Him to be the one whom the Zacchaeuses of today encounter. I too, even while working on this book—I am a priest, after all—asked myself what it really means these days to bring someone closer to Christ, and, through Christ, closer to God. I don't think it is quite as easy as certain enthusiastic Christians believe. A priest must not become an agitator, a propagandist, someone with pat slogans who is skilled at manipulating others. His role should be to accompany others, to "put them in the picture," to bring them to the gates of mystery, rather than to "win them over" in the way that politicians or traders draw attention to their latest wares.

This must be also apparent in the way we address others. It must be audible and discernible from the very way we speak and the language we use. After all, our language is the fruit of our heart's persuasion. If our language is not empty prattle or mindless production of clichés, it is itself a deed that can do much good. In that sense, "by their fruits shall ye know them" applies to the very way we speak.

Maybe the time has come for us to abandon much of the "pious vocabulary" we use in our discourse and on our banners. It has lost its full meaning for us with constant and often careless use. Other words have become too heavy, stiff, and corroded; they have become too cumbersome to express the message of the Gospel—the joyful news. Some of our pious expressions are already like a "burst drum" and no longer capable of singing God's praises—"incapable of dancing," as Nietzsche expected of a God he could believe in. Nietzsche, who came from a line of pastors, ruthlessly diagnosed in our sermons "the spirit of heaviness," and above all *"moraline,"* the poison of pessimistic, embittered moralizing. That haughtily sullen *specious gravity,* betraying a lack of humor and spontaneity and an insufficient inner freedom, has always reminded me of Michal, the daughter of Saul, who scorned King David when he danced before the ark of the covenant. This kind of piety tends to be punished by barrenness, as was Michal.

Yet David's dance before the ark had nothing in common with the showmanship of the professional entertainers in the present-day religious circus. I remember first watching a megashow of an evangelical preacher on American TV and hoping for a long time that it was just a comedy program caricaturing religion. I didn't want to believe that someone could seriously believe that it is possible to talk about God with such vulgar matter-of-factness and propagate the Gospel as if it were some reliable brand of automobile. Spiritual joy was replaced there by a cheap surrogate: entertainment—kitsch pandering to the taste of the unthinking consumers of today's mass "entertainment industry." It is truly sad to observe how those who ought to be prophets are transformed into embarrassing clowns.

Prophets should be a people of truth. But the truth of the Gospel is not the same as the truth of a scientific theory (in the sense that the truth of science has been understood by the advocates of scientism and positivism). It cannot be confined in definitions and conflict-free closed systems. Jesus linked forever after three concepts—the truth, the way, and life. Truth, like the way and life, is in constant movement and process, although this process cannot be construed as unidirectional development and progress. The Bible leads us to the truth, not by means of definitions or theoretical systems, but through stories, through dramas both large and small—such as the story of Zacchaeus and thousands more. The best way for us to understand the biblical stories is *to enter into them,* to become involved in those dramas—at the very least like the participants in the sacred dramas of ancient Greece—and experience through them catharsis, our own transformations.

If we want to talk about divine matters these days, we have to heal certain words and resurrect them, because they have become exhausted under the weight of the many different meanings that people have imposed on them over the centuries. This project brings to mind the lines of an old church hymn, a burning supplication to the Spirit of God: warm that which is cold, moisten that which is dry from fever, heal that which is sick, move that which is rigid. And maybe we could add another appeal: bring closer that which is distant!

CHAPTER 2

ↄ

Blessed Are the Distant

It is not fortuitous that Zacchaeus wasn't part of the crowds. Even
though, as a chief tax collector, Zacchaeus held an important and lu-
crative position, he was a person *on the fringe of society,* like the blind
beggar at the edge of the road to Jericho, whom Jesus had healed
just before meeting him. He was alienated from his neighbors by the
very fact of being a customs officer, i.e., someone performing a job
that was shunned for political, national, ritual, and moral reasons.
Customs officers collected taxes for the hated occupying power,
handled coins that bore the emperor's likeness—money that a pious
Jew, according to the teachings of rigorous rabbis, should not even
touch. And on top of that, they would line their pockets illegally.
Zacchaeus was despised by his fellow countrymen, although they
may also have envied him, since he was, as it is written, a very
wealthy man.

Jesus's conversation with Zacchaeus is not an isolated incident
in the New Testament. One might even describe it as a kind of
"Gospel in miniature," in which we discover in a few concise sentences an accurate picture and illustration of Jesus's mission of converting, healing, finding, and welcoming his "lost sheep." That

probably explains why this passage became a favorite theme of sermons and essays by some of the great Christian thinkers, such as St. Ambrose, St. Albert the Great, Erasmus, and Martin Luther—as well as of thousands of artistic representations, from the early Christian sarcophagi to the *evangeliars* of the German emperors Otto II and Henry II, the medieval frescoes in the church of Sant'Angelo in Formis, the psalter in the Pantokrator Monastery on Mount Athos—and wherever else we encounter the figure of the little tax official.

Jesus never stopped searching out those who were "distant." In His parables, the rabbi from Nazareth habitually ascribed positive roles to scorned groups such as the Samaritans, detested customs officials, prostitutes, and other sinners. He devoted Himself to lepers, the physically handicapped, and others who were excluded from society. His interest did not derive from any romantic predilection for the "lower depths," or from angry youthful revolt against the status quo, and not even, for that matter, from "social welfare" or political solidarity with the poor, the oppressed, and the exploited, as we understand it nowadays. At the center of His attention alongside the poor were the sick, "sinners" of every kind, and also rich customs officials and tax collectors like Zacchaeus. (Note that even after Zacchaeus's conversion, Jesus didn't urge him to abandon his profession, and we are not obliged to assume that Zacchaeus sank into poverty after making his promised recompense for wrongs done.) What they all have in common is that they are all—for various reasons—*on the fringes* of the setting in which Jesus worked, one that largely defies categorizations under our familiar headings of state, nation, or church, and is most frequently described in the New Testament as "this world."

In the light of his presence, the world that Jesus entered appeared sickly, empty, and inward-looking—a world *without heart.* Those who occupied the highest positions in it had *hearts of stone, not of flesh;* their hearts were *uncircumcised* and *waxed gross;* they were like *whited sepulchers,* full of uncleanness. In such a world, many people felt abandoned *like sheep without a shepherd.* And Jesus Himself cannot find a home in such a world; he has nowhere to lay his head.[1] That is another reason why he speaks above all to "people on the fringes" and identifies with them.[2]

Jesus lives in a state of constant tension with individuals, groups, institutions, and symbols that constitute the center, the elite of that society—such as the temple and the priests around it, the religious judges and dignitaries, those who "have taken their seat on the chair of Moses," above all the scribes and the Pharisees who incarnated moral and intellectual authority. Eventually, He comes into fatal conflict with the political power of the Roman empire, even though He Himself avoided such a confrontation.

In his best seller *What Jesus Meant,* Garry Wills is undoubtedly right to describe Jesus as an explicit opponent of the "religion of the temple elite"—Israel's spiritual center at that time—and to interpret in the same vein, not only the well-known scene of Jesus and the money changers, but also several other passages in the Gospels, including the cursing of the barren fig tree and His subsequent avowal that "this mountain"—the Temple Mount!—could be lifted up and thrown into the sea by the faith of His disciples (Mark 11:22–24). It's no coincidence that that passage ends with a promise that prayers will be heard: faith and prayer are all that are required for communication with God; temple offerings are no longer necessary.[3] In John's Gospel, in much the same way, Jesus tells the Samaritan woman that the time is coming when there will be no need for temples, neither the one in Jerusalem nor the Samaritan one at Mount Gerizim, because true worshippers will worship the Father in *spirit and truth* (John 4:21–23).

Jesus's entire ministry, His teachings and His actions, could be characterized using Nietzsche's expression "reevaluating values." It is poignantly foreshadowed in Luke's Gospel by Mary's hymn to "God's revolution": "[God] has shown might with his arm, dispersed the arrogant of mind and heart. He has thrown down the rulers from their thrones but lifted up the lowly. The hungry He has filled with good things; the rich He has sent away empty" (Luke 1:51–53). Blessedness and its counterpart "woe" are expressed in similar paradoxes, such as His well-known statement that "the first will be last, and the last will be first" (Matt. 19:30).

Blessed are you on the fringes, for you shall be at the center, at the heart!—that could well sum up the bulk of what Jesus said and did. Jesus completely ignored much of what was normally regarded by other people to be the immovable center—this is particularly apparent in His attitude to the ritual provisions of the Law. And He placed at the center just one value, a value that was absolute for Him—love. And He invited everyone "on the fringes" to that center.

The Kingdom He came to proclaim, the promised eschatological future, which is to show itself in fullness at the end of time, is now *also here and now*—in Christ *through Him, with Him, and in Him.* That is the Good News of the Gospel. Those on the fringes are now at the center, because Jesus sat at one table with them and took them into His heart. But His heart may be more hidden than one might think from some pious paintings. "Where your treasure is, there also

will your heart be," Jesus says (Luke 12:34). And doesn't His treasure consist precisely of all those *people on the fringes*—including those
doubters and seekers?

ॐ

Throughout the history of the church, solidarity with the poor and
socially deprived, care for the sick and handicapped, and courage to
stand up for the oppressed, the exploited, and the persecuted, have
been part and parcel of Christian witness in this world, and maybe
it is now more necessary than ever before. By performing such
things, by being the salt of the earth and by bringing the scent of
heaven to the dark and malodorous corners of the earth, one can be
sure of walking in the footsteps of Christ and the thousands of saints
of the past.

However, as I meditated on Jesus's encounter with Zacchaeus
and the many other examples of His "prior interest in people on the
fringes," it struck me that perhaps something extra was needed today
in order to fully follow in Christ's footsteps: an interest, or better still
a *prior interest,* in people *on the fringes of faith,* in those who remain in
the anteroom of the church, should they actually come that close to
it. It is an interest in people in the "gray zone" between religious
certainty and atheism, an interest in the doubters and seekers.

Of course, missionaries of almost every religion, church, and
sect already fish these waters of the "seekers." And many *priests,
scribes, and Pharisees* of today would no doubt praise my interest.
However, my interest in these people on the fringes is not of the
narrowly missionary variety. My chief interest is not to "convert"
them, not to bring "certainty" to the uncertain.[4]

There is naturally a need for teaching, for persuasion and conversion, and for providing answers to the questions from seekers; after all, Jesus Himself healed the sick and directed the hungry to be filled. The injunction "to teach the ignorant" is also to be found on the traditional list of "Spiritual Works of Mercy." But as we shall see, Jesus did not fill all the hungry (indeed, He refused to turn stones into bread for that purpose as a devilish temptation), and He did not bring the marginalized into the center by means of social revolution in order to make them powerful and wealthy. He did not provide good entertainment for the mourner or heaven on earth for the persecuted, let alone a just society in the near future or the enticing prospect of a life without risks, obstacles, or crosses. He proclaimed that the poor, the mourners, and the persecuted were *blessed.* That master of paradox congratulated them.

Jesus blessed the poor—not in order to keep the poor in their place by offering them an opiate promise of reward in the afterlife, as some Marxists interpret that passage (and as some Christians actually represented it from time to time). He made poverty *a metaphor of openness* toward God's gifts. It is necessary to preserve *poverty of the spirit,* and not join the ranks of the full, the sure, and self-assured, who are satisfied and locked within themselves.

Similarly, in terms of the spirit, I believe it is necessary to preserve a *spirit of seeking.* (Eastern spiritual masters use the term "beginner's mind.") I have nothing against missions and preaching. Preaching is necessary in the same way that feeding the hungry is necessary. But this is a different issue: one must *maintain a seeking spirit,* just as one must have a spirit of poverty—it is necessary to *remain open* because only in that way may we reach the Kingdom of God. It is in this sense that Jesus blesses these poor, the mourning, and those who thirst after righteousness; He does not cynically congratulate them because their pockets and stomachs are empty and their faces tear-stained.

Care for and closeness to the poor are not beneficial just to them, but *also to us*; They enable us to teach in the spirit of poverty and to preserve it. And our closeness to the seekers ought also to teach us openness; we don't have to solely think about having to teach and edify them—*we can also learn a great deal from them*. And we can try to show those people in the church who are self-assured and "satiated" about their religion that it is necessary, at least sometimes, to reach out to people on the fringe of the churches—and not just to "convert" and assimilate them. Being able to take a look at how God appears from the standpoint of people who are searching, doubting, and questioning—isn't this a new, exciting, necessary, and useful *religious experience*?

ॐ

Liberation theology issued a very important challenge: to read the Gospel with the eyes of the poor. Its proponents called for scripture and witness of the tradition to be read *from the standpoint of the poor*, as a message for the poor, which can be understood authentically only by those who are themselves poor or who demonstrate active solidarity with the poor. And in that spirit they proposed a fresh examination and reinterpretation of theology as a whole.

Yet we can now offer another, different hermeneutic rule, another key to a fresh understanding of scripture and the Christian message: it is necessary to read scripture and live the faith also *from the standpoint of our profound solidarity with people who are religiously seeking, and, if need be, with those who experience God's hiddenness and transcendence "from the other side."* We must hear Jesus's call "with the ears of Zacchaeus"! We must look at him from the viewpoint of Zacchaeus's hiding place and distance—which is also, however, a place of observation and expectation.

This "new theology of liberation" ought to be a theology of *inner* liberation—liberation from "certainties" regarding religion, whether these are the certainties of an atheism that does not question itself or certainties of a religiosity that has similarly petrified on the surface. Paul Tillich maintained that the main dividing line runs, not between those who regard themselves as believers and those who regard themselves as nonbelievers, but between those whom God leaves indifferent—whether "indifferent atheists" or conventional Christians—and those who are existentially concerned by the "question of God"—whether they be passionate seekers after God (such as mystics), people "wrestling with God" (like Nietzsche), or people who thirst after faith but are unable to find a place in any form of religion they have so far encountered.

In the same way that the church must shed ostentation in order to undertake missionary activity in the world of the socially poor, it must shed many of its certainties if it is to enter the world of religious insecurity. It must get rid of not only the outward signs of baroque triumphalism—as the last Council encouraged it to do—but above all the inward monopolistic triumphalism of being the sole repository of the truth. I also think it useful or even essential at the present time, when various kinds of commercial religiosity offer their wares so attractively, to take seriously the fact that God *is not so "readily available."* If we can understand those who are confronted with a silent, hidden, or distant God—including those who have been led to reject religion because of that experience—it can help us achieve a more mature form of faith than the naive and vulgar theism that is rightly criticized by atheists. In the same way that Latin American theology introduced the concept of "sinful structures" into theology, even into papal documents, so also our theology of liberation should highlight the "sinfulness" of certain structures of thinking and speaking, as well as the many "religious stereotypes" that damage faith and result in isolation from God: from the naive "proving God" to a certain kind of theodicy ("justifying God" in the face of evil and misfortune), which, in the words of J. B. Metz, tends to have the effect of an attempt "to reach agreement with God behind the backs of the suffering members of humanity."

Latin American liberation theology confronted the situation in the "Third World" and undoubtedly ensured that theology transcended its "Atlantic horizon." It thus assisted the development of a contextual theology and helped theologians reflect on the fact that their thinking is limited by attitudes determined by place and time, by the society and the culture in which they live and work. "A new liberation theology" of *inner liberation,* by contrast, should address the Western world and its largely unique phenomenon of secularism and modern atheism.

An inexhaustible source of inspiration for this type of theological reflection—a source, moreover, that almost all the great mystics, as well as the ancient theologians, including Thomas Aquinas, drew on—will undoubtedly be so-called *negative theology* (or apophatic theology), which constitutes a kind of "underground current" of Christian theology. It maintains that the surest way to reach God is by the path of negation, by the denial of all positive testimonials of Him, because God transcends the scope of our thinking, imagination, and language to such a degree that the most we can say about Him is what He is not; attempts to express "what He is" can lead to the creation of idols. From the perspective of this mystic theology—as Paul Tillich knew well—one might even say that a certain type of atheism—"denial of God"—tends to bring God closer rather than distance Him.

In a lecture some time ago, I sketched out an analogous concept of "negative eschatology."[5] We often hear that traditional attitudes connected with Christian teaching about "last things" are in crisis and a great deal of "secular eschatologies" arrive to fill the vacuum (often very dangerous ones, such as the Marxist concept of communist society). Indeed, two eschatological visions recently emerged from Harvard, and they provoked widespread comment throughout the world: Huntington's theory of the "clash of civilizations" and Fukuyama's theory about "the end of history," i.e., the global victory of liberal democracy. It is my view that this is precisely the moment for Christian theology to point to the last horizon of our expectations: "the absolute future" (to use one of Rahner's favorite expressions) as a mystery truly transcending all our notions. It is necessary to negate these notions (the projections of our own yearnings and fears), whether religious or secular in essence, in the same way that negative theology negates notions about God. At the same time, however, we must nurture our openness toward this inconceivable absolute future. Such a concept of "negative eschatology" would have a dual function: on the one hand, to be a critical thorn vis-à-vis attempts by various ideologies to absolutize their own projects, and on the other, to be a thorn of a hope and "holy restlessness" that would remind society and the church that their present state (including the state of their knowledge) is only provisional, that it is not the summit where they might sleep in self-satisfied sloth.

By the middle of the nineteenth century, Kierkegaard had already advanced a new type of religious thinking: a philosophical theology that was not "study of God," but instead a hermeneutics of the existential experience of faith—or, put another way, of faith as the most radical existential experience. We should undoubtedly draw on that tradition. Out of all theological disciplines, that theological current is probably closest to spiritual theology; after all, spirituality is without doubt the dimension of Christian faith most relevant to the spiritual climate of present-day Western society. However, if the theological impulses I have indicated are embodied in a lived faith and spirituality, then this *liberation spirituality* or *exodus spirituality* should not lead to shirking our responsibility for the society in which we have been placed. On the contrary, one of its essential tasks is sensitivity to the *signs of the times* in the cultural and political climate of today's world. "Solidarity with seekers" implies sharing in their seeking and questioning.

As I reflect here, in the silence of the hermitage, on which people and ideas could provide building blocks or inspiration for the kind of theology and spirituality that I believe is needed in our time, there comes to mind one of the best-known hermits of the last century: the American convert who subsequently became a Trappist, an author of influential books on spiritual life, and a pioneer of interreligious dialogue—Thomas Merton. Merton also did not simply yearn, but strove practically—in the spirit and style of the 1960s, with all their left-wing political illusions—to link contemplation and action, to introduce the impulses of liberation theology into spirituality and offer the path of a spiritual life, which would also embody responsibility for the present-day world and be a step in the direction of "others." The particular "others" with whom Merton felt profound solidarity, especially toward the end of his life, were pilgrims along the spiritual paths of the East—and the task of maintaining and enhancing interreligious dialogue undoubtedly remains one of our most important tasks today. But let us not allow our fascination with the exotic Far East lead us to ignore those distant "others" that we meet day in and day out on the streets of our own cities, and in our own universities, clubs, and workplaces.

The very last sentence that Thomas Merton spoke in this world, according to the testimony of Father de Grunne, who spoke with him in Bangkok just before his tragic death, was: "What we are asked to do today is not so much to speak about Christ as to let him live in us so that people may find him by feeling how he lives in us."[6] So let us go on asking how we can allow the one who was able to call Zacchaeus (and Merton, and the author of this present book, as well as many others) *by name,* and make distant people live convincingly in us.

CHAPTER 3

✣

Far from All Suns

While I was reflecting on the "people on the fringes," on solidarity with doubters, and on where, in fact, we might identify the center and the fringe of a body as remarkable as the church, I recalled a young woman who once wrote in her diary the words: *My vocation is to be love at the heart of the church.*

For many years, St. Thérèse de Lisieux was of marginal interest to me. I recall that it was on her feast day—although it had not been chosen expressly for that reason—that I started my systematic preparation for ordination in the "underground church." I waited in St. Ignatius's Church in Prague for a man I was to recognize by an agreed sign, who was to be my guide on that journey for many years preceding my ordination. I remember well what went on not only within me, but also around me—and remember also the well-known chocolate-box statue of St. Thérèse, with roses in her arms, before which—it being her feast day—a large candle burned.

What did I know about St. Thérèse at that time? I was aware of her only through sickly-sweet statues and pictures redolent of nineteenth-century religiosity. I expect I had little time in those days for her words and her mission within the church; there had been plenty of pious nuns whose diaries were full of sentimental sighs about love! After all, these days we tend to interpret such confessions and groans chiefly in terms of Freud's theory about the sublimation of the libido.

When I first read about the "little way" or the "way of childhood" taught by St. Thérèse, I came upon a remark of hers—no doubt uttered at some disagreeable and distressful moment, such as she seems to have endured frequently in the convent—that she gave God the freedom to treat her as a child treats its plaything: can a plaything reproach a child for ignoring it at a particular moment or for forgetting it in a corner? That was enough for me! "We're supposed to be playthings in God's hands? And God is supposed to be some forgetful child?" I said to myself, immediately closing the book in disgust, determined not to waste time on such infantile metaphors, and returning to the Heidegger I had started to read. Years later I found myself in a particular situation, when—with no disrespect to Heidegger—I found that statement of Thérèse's more helpful to me than *Sein und Zeit.* I realized how much self-disparagement it contained, beneficial humor that helped confront the temptation to pity oneself at moments of failure, to speculate fruitlessly on why God permits this or that to happen, why He fails to protect someone as excellent as me, to furtively cast the blame on everyone around, including God Himself.

But that was only the beginning of my "adventure with Thérèse." I gradually became more and more fascinated with this woman whom John Paul II proclaimed a "doctor of the church"—even though she left behind her no theological treatise and even her theological education was questionable to say the least. I read many of her texts and her biographies, and eventually I made a pilgrimage to her tomb. The photograph of her face has a permanent place on my writing desk.

When, a few years ago, I completed a book that provocatively defended "little faith" in contrast to "great," "unshakable," and self-assured faith (and I'll come back to those ideas at the end of this book), it was a great lesson in meekness for me when I subsequently learned that I had not discovered anything that was outlandishly novel. The thing that once persuaded me to make my spiritual home in Christianity and the Roman Catholic Church—namely the fact that it was a *religion of paradoxes*—and what I, in the footsteps of Pascal, Kierkegaard, Chesterton, and Graham Greene, had pondered on and described in such a complicated way, had been discovered, experienced, and described in her own distinctive language and style by that "Little Flower." My beliefs were, in fact, her "little way" viewed from a different angle, her path of spiritual childhood, which truly has nothing in common with infantility, although it often tends to be presented and propagated as such.

In a lecture I gave some years ago, I compared that "Little Flower" to Friedrich Nietzsche and called these two very different spiritual contemporaries "siblings"; I really had no idea at the time that I was not the first or by far the only one to have come up with that comparison. (Moreover, in view of my predilection for paradoxes, my occasional discovery that I have "figured out" something that some wise person had figured out before me fills me with an ideally paradoxical sense of satisfaction and frustration, pride and humility at the same time.)

Nietzsche and Thérèse both lived in the self-confident nineteenth-century world of science and progress, which, though few realized it at the time, was full of illusions and naïveté and would soon be superseded. It was also a time of piety, which was both sweetly sentimental and full of lugubrious moralizing, rigors, acquisition of merit, and cultivation of virtues (that pious version of the old Pelagian heresy), and of an obsessively neurotic fascination with sin. And Nietzsche and Thérèse both—albeit in very different ways and circumstances—turned their backs on those features of their time and on the subtle temptations within its spiritual climate.

Before her death, the young Carmelite nun experienced great spiritual conflicts and inner darkness. In that *night of trial,* her impending death once appeared to her—as she literally states—as a *night of nothingness.* "I no longer believe in eternal life: I feel that there is nothing beyond this mortal life," the doctor of the church wrote. "My mind is gripped by the arguments of the worst materialists" was another of her authentic statements. Not only was Thérèse to know the collapse of the sweet life of piety, which she had always known up to then; her previous profound sense of God's closeness was to be swallowed up by mist, darkness, and emptiness. She found herself "far from all suns," if I may be allowed to describe her experience in the words that Nietzsche's madman uses in his torrent of suggestive metaphors that sum up the death of God.[1] Thérèse describes how Christ led her into a subterranean space "where no sun shines any longer."

When one is on the verge of death, it is no doubt unexceptional, even for those with a deep belief, to undergo similar trials, as if they were participating in the painful mystery of Christ's death throes, which we can only slightly sense from His cry of "My God, my God, why have you forsaken me"—a cry that only one of the Evangelists had the courage to record. But there is something else at issue here. Mother Agnes, who held the final conversations with the dying Thérèse and was the first editor (and eager censor) of her writings, construed Thérèse's mental state (in the tradition of Carmelite mysticism) as a "dark night of the spirit"—and she formulated her statements accordingly—but thereby she failed to grasp what was truly original, new, and unique about Thérèse de Lisieux, something that, understandably, is absent in the case of both the "great Theresa" of Avila and John of the Cross.

"Little Thérèse's" principle was *"to accept even the strangest thoughts"* out of love for God. What is therefore most remarkable about Thérèse is the way she accepted and perceived her contest with God, with darkness and forlornness, her experience with the absence of God and the eclipse of her faith. She accepted it as *a mark of solidarity with unbelievers.*

This young woman, who had grown up in a small-town household that was more bigoted than pious, and who did not even liberate herself from those surroundings when she entered a convent (which her three sisters had also entered in turn), had probably never seen an atheist at close quarters in her life. She writes in her diary that prior to that fateful Easter of 1896—when her hemorrhaging on Good Friday caused her to realize that she herself was already nailed to the cross of an incurable disease and close to death—*she did not believe that there existed any atheists.* She had simply considered them to be people who "contradicted their own convictions." (Indeed, that is how, even now, millions of people outside Western civilization continue to react when they hear about atheists: they cannot even imagine that such an attitude is possible.)

But then—she continues—Christ revealed to her that there really were people who lived entirely without faith. And that fact— that atheism was not simply an "illusion" or sinful self-delusion and deception of others, and had to be taken very seriously—was confirmed when she was deprived of her own certainty of faith. She could no longer benefit from her previous religious certainties, she could not enjoy the light and joy of a childlike faith. One of her biographers notes that the word *"jouissance,"* enjoyment, which she uses here, genuinely meant in the language of her day being able to use some property, to get pleasure from the ownership of something; Thérèse would no longer *have* faith, would no longer *possess* its assurance.[2]

Thérèse declares that she *perceives unbelievers as her brothers,* with whom she *sits at the same table and eats the same bread*—and she begs Jesus not to banish her therefrom. Unlike them, she is aware of the *bitterness* of this bread, because, unlike them, she has known the joy of God's closeness (even though the memory of it now only deepens her pain), whereas people indifferent to God are generally quite unaware of the burden and tragedy of their situation. In fact, it is only thanks to her previous experience of faith that she is able to experience in depth the real drama of abandonment by God, as well as discover and experience the hidden face of atheism, which many accept with such casual matter-of-factness. (In like manner—as we shall see later—Nietzsche's *madman* comes among those *who don't believe in God* and fail to see any problem with the atheism that they now take for granted, in order to reveal to them the real nature and consequence of their *killing of God.*)

Such an attitude to unbelievers was alien to the church of her day, which regarded atheism as error, delusion, and above all sin. There were possibly some nuns who prayed for the unbelievers and made sacrifices for them out of a desire to be *mothers* to them and the godparents of their conversion. Thérèse, on the other hand, wanted to be their *sister* and regarded them explicitly as her brothers.[3]

The French church at that period was absorbed in desperate defensive action against burgeoning atheism. The more it failed to realize and acknowledge the extent to which its dry-as-dust theology contributed to the secularism of its age, the more desperately it sought out external enemies and their undercover agents within its own ranks. Everything was the fault of a worldwide conspiracy of Jews and Freemasons. (In that same period, Drumont waved the flag of militant anti-Semitism and nationalism, and the "bible of anti-Semitism" by Gougenot des Mousseaux was read avidly; Freemasonry was regarded as "a tool of Judaism for destroying Christianity and establishing the church of Satan.") A paranoid campaign against "modernism" was unleashed within the church, rejecting any other approach to modern thinking but "circular defense." At a time when many priests were writing apologetic treatises and preaching outraged sermons against atheism—either because it was part of the job or because it drowned out their own doubts—this young woman from Normandy *was showing solidarity with atheists* in a remarkable way and seeing atheism as a cup of pain, from which she now drank deeply in her own night of Gethsemane.

In François Mauriac's *Life of Jesus,* where he describes Jesus praying at Gethsemane, perspiring blood while the apostles sleep, he writes: "The Son of Man became a pendulum between man's torpor and God's absence—from the absent Father to the sleeping friend." Thérèse likewise became a pendulum between an unbelieving world and a deaf heaven—and that is her message, *that is the lesson of this doctor of the church of our times.*

Only from that site of uncertainty can fall the "rain of grace," the rain of roses that Thérèse is said to have promised to send to the earth and with which she is depicted on those sugary kitsch statues in almost every Catholic church on the planet. These are no artificial flowers, no perfumed paper roses: *there is no rose without thorns.*

Last year I read what is perhaps the most thorough and in-depth biography of St. Thérèse, from the pen of the American theologian Thomas Nevin.[4] Free of the sweetly pious icing of previous editions, the author, who had carefully studied Thérèse's authentic and unexpurgated texts, came to the convincing if somewhat shocking conclusion that this saint and doctor of the church *died without faith,* literally without belief in heaven and eternal life. And Nevin does not limit himself solely to an analysis of the mental states of the dying woman; his subject represents a more serious and universal theological problem.[5] Is there something that can "replace faith" when it dies on the cross of our pains, doubts, and unanswered questions?

On the verge of death, Thérèse confesses that she has "lost her faith" and all her certainty and light—*she is now only capable of loving.* She "does not see" God in the light of faith, but nonetheless she relates to Him with a passionate love. Suddenly her youthful decision that her vocation was to be *love in the heart of the church* loses all hint of sentimentality. God is terribly distant; the dying woman experiences only unfathomable emptiness. She is incapable of filling it with faith, because in the mist her faith has lost its "subject"; it is like the bridge at Avignon that did not reach the other bank. And yet, in the depths of her suffering, there remains the thing to which she dedicated herself on the brink of adulthood, and which she patiently exercised even when she confronted various expressions of spite on the part of her sisters in the convent—patient love. "Love is patient, love is kind. It is not jealous. . . . It endures all things," writes the apostle Paul.[6]

At the gates of death, did Thérèse perhaps experience something of that final state of which St. Paul writes in his letter to the Corinthians—that ultimate state when everything will come to nothing? Perhaps his words also apply to faith and hope, for they will have "fulfilled their task" of accompanying us in the valley of shadow of this ambiguous world—but love will endure?[7] Was the hell of Thérèse's suffering and inner darkness paradoxically the entrance to a "heaven," where just one of the three divine virtues survives?

Thérèse is a master of paradox; her "little way" is, quite simply, a paradox that thoroughly engrossed her, the paradox familiar from the letters of St. Paul: great things are revealed in small things; God's wisdom is revealed in human foolishness (and vice versa); God's strength is revealed in human weakness. Thérèse taught a faith that is creative because it can *reinterpret life situations* and find a new, hidden, deeper meaning in them—one that is often the antithesis of how those situations appear to the outward gaze.

Whereas the church of her day preached a dread of sin and a systematic ascent to ultimate virtue and spiritual and moral perfection, Thérèse—fully in the spirit of St. Paul's letters—taught the need to accept with joy and thankfulness one's own weakness as a space that God's kindness and mercy may enter (while haughty virtue refuses admittance). She writes that those who have been climbing the hill of virtue for a long time ought to accept with humble joy their own collapse and (God-willed) fall, because God awaits them not at the dreamed-of "heights" but precisely at the very bottom, "deep in the fertile valley of humility."

At a time when spiritual leaders were teaching believers to collect, count, and carefully record their good deeds, Thérèse firmly rejected that sort of accounting: *I count nothing.* I simply do everything out of love—and if I then stand empty-handed and utterly poor in the ranks of those who collected, counted, and recorded their merits, isn't that, after all, the poverty that Christ speaks about in the Sermon on the Mount: Blessed are the poor?

Hans Urs von Balthasar describes this young nun (who was photographed dressed as Joan of Arc, interpreting the role of her favorite heroine in a play at the convent) as a born warrior, whose texts teem with symbols of battle: she fought against everything in which she sensed a continuation of the Pharisees, "against that will-to-power disguised in the mantle of religion that drives one to assert one's own greatness instead of acknowledging that God alone is great . . . against every ascetical practice which aims not at God but at one's own 'perfection,' and which is nothing more than spiritual beauty treatment."[8]

Thérèse seeks in that vein to *reinterpret* even her painful experience of abandonment by God as a special gift and challenge—but also as a cross beneath which her knees buckle; she, after all, refused the endeavors of her sisters to depict her death as "heroic suffering" in the spirit of the kitsch biographies of the saints. And the fact that she interprets her states of abandonment by God as sharing a table with unbelievers means that she also creates scope to *reinterpret their atheism*: what they accept with indifference and as a matter of fact (like those people in the market addressed by Nietzsche's "madman") is actually a state of darkness "far from all suns."

For Nietzsche, looking into the abyss that opens up after the "death of God" represented an opportunity and challenge to fill the resultant space with a new type of humanity: the superman. In the case of Thérèse, we may assume that she would construe her experience with this abyss traditionally as a sacrifice, aimed at helping bring sinful unbelievers back into the bosom of the church—and naturally we would find texts by her (and I don't intend here to enter into the rather complex issue of the extent to which we can recognize Thérèse's authentic voice beneath the censorship, misinterpretations, and retouching of her pious editors) that suggest such an interpretation.

It would then not be surprising if atheists were to reject Thérèse's interpretation of the hidden face of their atheism as an "unsolicited favor," as a romantic projection of her own image, which does not respect them, their self-understanding, their distinctiveness, and their right to be themselves, but rather attempts to manipulate them (maybe even by some kind of emotional blackmail) into coming back to where they do not want to go.

However, if I am correct in my understanding of Thérèse and of her path through paradox and constant reinterpretation, then her concern was something else: not simply to draw these unbelievers back into the heart of the church, but rather to broaden that heart by including their experience of darkness. Through her solidarity with unbelievers, she conquers *new territory* (along with its inhabitants) for a church that has previously been too closed.

Thérèse inspires us to a faith that does not retreat cowardly to the strongholds of its certainties when confronted by the challenge of atheism, that does not fire the arguments of militant apologists across the trenches at atheism from a safe position, but instead goes "unarmed" with much greater courage—as St. Francis once did into the sultan's camp—into the "camp of unbelievers" and brings therefrom a new "trophy" for the treasure-house of faith: the atheists' experience with a distant God. By now, the existential "truth of atheism," that experience of pain that was previously the "rock of atheism," is also part of the *treasure-house of faith*. Faith construed this way and lived authentically and patiently in the depth of night now carries an existential experience within itself. It lacks nothing of what is part of the human condition. It endures people's night also.

The fact that Thérèse is "love at the heart of the church," a love that glows even in the night of faith, that endures even where faith "has died," proves that this love—and hence also the mysterious "heart of the church," its deep, hidden dimension—is much broader, deeper, and more openhanded than it previously seemed or seems from outside. There is a place here even for those whose certainties (and above all "religious certainties") have been shaken, uprooted, or thrust into darkness. Aren't these people in fact just one step from that blessed spiritual poverty, "deprivation," of which Meister Eckhart spoke, which means "to know nothing, have nothing, be nothing"?

The dialectic of emptiness and satiety is familiar to many mystics—and not just Christian ones. Only this poverty can God fill completely. Only from the depths of this abyss can one glimpse "the breadth and length and height and depth, and . . . know the love of Christ that surpasses knowledge" that Paul writes about (Eph. 3:19). If love overtakes faith on the path to the final goal and even survives "the death of faith," then it is capable of embracing nonbelievers too, and their unbelief. I'll state here what will be evident from various angles in the deliberations of this book: *faith can overcome unbelief only by embracing it.*

Yes, Thérèse is rightly the teacher of the church of our time, even though she wrote no theological treatise. Her experience of

God's distance and her relationship to nonbelievers is perhaps more topical for us than the many-volumed works of other doctors of the faith and fathers of the church. "Little Thérèse" shows us more clearly than other saints where the heart of the church is, and what happens within it. She can bring to the very heart of the church something that we need urgently to learn, now of all times.

ふん

Hans Urs von Balthasar noticed striking parallels between Thérèse's stress on grace (in contrast to the then-widespread emphasis on deeds, merits, the cultivation of "perfection," and ascetic exercises) and the concerns of Luther and the reformers. And he adds a remarkable note: "It is Luther's error to have profaned mystical truths, which presuppose an intimate exchange of love between God and man, by treating them as general formulae for the sinner's relation to God. . . . Thérèse's mistake is to have restricted the whole drama between God and the soul to what happened in her own exceptional case."[9] That is all von Balthasar has to say about the matter.

Luther's mystical "tower experience" gave rise to a theology of justification on the basis of a trusting faith; what has remained in the church's memory from Thérèse's mystic experiences is the "little path" as one style of private spirituality, a personal path to spiritual maturity. Hasn't the time come for Thérèse's spiritual path, and particularly "solidarity with unbelievers," to be an inspiration as a hermeneutic key *toward new theological reflection on present-day society, its spiritual climate, and the church's mission at the present time?*

Does this not suggest a new and yet unused path to meet in a much more radical way than ever before the challenge of the last

Vatican Council: to engage in dialogue with the atheism of our time—i.e., to utterly de-demonize "unbelievers" and reinterpret at least a certain kind of "unbelief" as a view "from the other side" of the steep, "cloud-covered" mountain peak of the impenetrable divine mystery? To show atheism not as a *lie*, but as an *incomplete truth*? To show living faith not as a set of dusty precepts, but as a path of maturation that even includes valleys of "the silence of God"—but that, unlike the purveyors of "certainties," does not circumvent them or abandon any further search but patiently moves on.

"De-demonizing unbelievers" means fulfilling the rule that it is necessary to "distinguish the sin from the sinner." Is atheism a sin? Yes—but more in the sense of a *debt* (as in earlier translations of the Lord's Prayer, or as in various languages where the word for sin and the word for debt are the same—the Latin *debitum* or the German *Schuld*). It is unfinished work, an unresolved matter, an uncompleted building. It is an unfinished and therefore unpalatable dish that needs a dash of the salt of faith. Atheism is a useful antithesis to naive, vulgar theism—but it is necessary to take a further step toward synthesis and mature belief. Mature belief involves breathing out and breathing in, night and day; atheism is simply a fragment.

But we must not fall prey to triumphalism or pride in these reflections—we must be aware that even "mature belief" remains unfinished business as far as we are concerned (and if we are to complete the task we need to take seriously the experience of atheism), rather than something that we already possess and could consider our "property." We too have yet to fulfill the challenge of the Letter to the Hebrews: "Let us leave behind the basic teaching about Christ and advance to maturity. . . . And we shall do this, if only God permits" (Heb. 6:1–3).

✌

As I reflect on Thérèse's spiritual kinship with those at a distance, another comparison occurs to me. The fact is often tactfully ignored nowadays that, in the course of his hectic revivalist work, St. Maximilian Kolbe, priest of the Conventual Franciscan order and martyr of Auschwitz, was consumed by a similar spirit of fanatical struggle against "Jew-Freemasons" that prevailed in nationalist and anti-Semitic circles of French Catholicism at St. Thérèse's time, the same dread of a Satan about to brandish the black flag of anarchy above St. Peter's Basilica in Rome. In the end, by a strange irony of history, God placed that "righteous Job"—by the hand of quite a different Satan than the one he expected: German National Socialism—into the hell of the Holocaust, so that he might show solidarity, not simply in spiritual visions but through his martyrdom, with the millions of Jews and other victims of Nazism, including Communists, liberals, and many other "infidels" whom he once so dreaded.

The night into which Maximilian Kolbe was thrust and in which he stood the test as a martyr of extreme love and solidarity—by volunteering to accept death in place of another prisoner—was not the same night of trial as the young dying nun's. Here the dark abyss "far from all suns"—the state of the world after the "death of God"—became a dreadful historical reality. "The dark night" had become a collective night, and it was not the only one, not just in a twentieth century that was so proud of its progressiveness and rationality, but also, it seems, in our own subsequent one.

A young girl from Normandy was sent into the darkness of what still tended to be an "intellectual atheism" of the late nineteenth century, while into the hell of Auschwitz—a satanic instrument for the liquidation of the chosen people—were sent that Polish priest and also a Jewish Carmelite nun, Edith Stein, who was a convert from modern intellectual culture. Inevitably the question arises: Who will be that light of God in the darkness of the rampant evil of "religious terrorism"? Who will God send to suffer this particularly refined form of alienation from God "in God's name"? Who will show Christians today that we must not answer violence solely with violence, nor invoke God's name in godless "holy wars," and how will they be shown? In what way, at these dramatic moments—and precisely now—are we to experience *solidarity with distant neighbors,* to distinguish the sin from the sinner, and to call sin by its proper name, while demonstrating to those who are most distant from us—not only in words but also deeds—*that we can call them brothers even though they do not want to see us in that way?*

It was no lesser a person than St. Augustine who told the Christians of his day, and tells us now: "The prophet refers to some men saying: *When they say to you, You are not our brothers, you are to tell them, You are our brothers. Consider whom he intended by these words.*" Yes, we must indeed consider, and consider seriously!

✸

But let us return for a moment to the sickbed of St. Thérèse. Perhaps one could demur that Thérèse did not lose her faith, that she merely lost that sense of religious certainty, of the certainty of God's closeness; that her faith was simply stripped bare like Jesus on the cross. One could recall that John of the Cross, the great teacher of her order, had described precisely that naked faith as the deepest and most authentic. One could stress that her faith was certainly not extinguished as in the case of those people who have recklessly "dissolved it in the world"—it was more a matter of her "dissolving it in love." But let us not try to be more pious than the saint herself or wiser than that doctor of the faith. Let us ask instead—as we have already indicated—whether her spiritual experience on the brink of life and death can be a "sign of the times" for us today.

Some of the eschatological visions of the New Testament, such as the words of St. Paul mentioned above and particularly the closing passages of Revelation, tell us clearly that there will be no religion in the heavenly kingdom; faith will have passed away and the temple will be no more.[10] Allow me to voice a question that struck me in this context, even though it may seem insane and blasphemous to some at first sight. (But didn't St. Thérèse herself say that out of love for God she was prepared to accept *even the strangest thoughts*?)

My question is: Isn't a certain type of loss of faith in our age a sort of "foretaste" of the heavenly kingdom? One could answer with a definite negative: at best, atheism can only be a satanic caricature of heaven. In heaven there will no longer be faith, but there will be the *visio beatifica,* the "beatific vision"; at last God will be seen face to face. There will be no temple there because Christ Himself, the apocalyptic lamb, will be its temple and its light.

Postmodernist philosopher Gianni Vattimo claims that the present secular society is filled with Christ's *kenosis*—His emptying of Himself in the sense of St. Paul's hymn[11]—and is thus the logical culmination of the history of Christianity and the "age of the Holy Spirit" prophesied by Joachim de Fiore.[12] Writer Gertrud von Le Fort hinted in her novels *Die Magdeburgische Hochzeit* (The Magdeburg Wedding) and *Die Abberufung der Jungfrau von Barby* (The

Ecstasy of the Virgin of Barby) that the destruction of churches at the time of the religious wars actually fulfilled in some way the vision of the mystics—particularly Meister Eckhart—that it was necessary to reach a vision of God "without images."

There are definitely as many types of atheism as there are of belief. There is frivolous atheism, which, like Esau, sells its heritage of faith for a mess of pottage. There is a "forgetting about God" that immediately crams the space vacated with substitute idols of every kind. There is a haughty atheism for which "God must not exist" lest He eclipse the immensity of the human ego that seeks to take control of the deity's throne: "If there were gods, how could I bear not to be a god?" There is a liberating atheism that has finally gotten rid of its imaginary god, its own projection, which terrorized it for years. There is also a sad and painful atheism: "I would like to believe, but there is so much bitterness within me because of my own suffering and the world's pain that I am unable to."

And akin to them is precisely the "loss of faith" that we have in mind: the death of faith on the cross of our world, the hour when the individual is plunged into inner and outer darkness, "far from all suns." That is how the cross appears from the viewpoint of our world. That is what the human individual looks like when the dark shadow of the cross falls upon him—many experienced it during particular historical events or at particular moments of their lives. The Gospel story and this kind of atheism intersect at the moment of Jesus's cry on the cross: "My God, why have you forsaken me?" Chesterton expresses it in a remarkable passage: "Let the atheists themselves choose a god. They will find only one divinity who ever uttered their isolation; only one religion in which God seemed for an instant to be an atheist."[13]

Nevertheless, the underlying message of the Gospel is that this is not the only possible prospect; this is not the last word. This is only "the truth of Good Friday," but after it—after the long, silent waiting of Holy Saturday—comes the morning that brings yet *another message,* no less truthful—although many overslept and missed that all-too-early morning.

St. John of the Cross, the mystic of the dark night of the soul, who was also a gifted poet, musician, and painter, left behind a drawing of the Crucifixion *seen from above,* from the perspective of the Father; it was this sketch that many centuries later inspired the painting by Salvador Dali. Seen from above, that dark moment appears quite differently: defeat is victory—this is the "death of death." Man does not fall into boundless darkness but returns home, into the full light of truth: faith has already fulfilled its pilgrim task; only love reigns there now. This will not *cancel faith but fulfill it*; if faith "dies," it does so only by being dissolved in love—but even this death may be experienced as a passage through the dark chasm of nothingness.

Christian faith—unlike "natural religiosity" and happy-go-lucky religiosity—is *resurrected faith,* faith that has to die on the cross, be buried, and rise again—in a *new form.* This faith is a process—and it is possible for people to find themselves at different phases of this process at different moments of their lives.

I have often heard the ironic comment that faith is simply "a crutch" to help those of us who are weak and lame, whereas the strong have no need of it. It is not "a crutch," but it might be compared to a pilgrim's staff that assists us on our journey through life. Maybe when someone is just about to cross the threshold of home, when the staff won't be needed anymore, it falls from his hands; it's not surprising if he loses his balance for a moment. "Seen from the other side"—from the viewpoint that we can only experience here as an assurance, as hope—beyond that threshold, at the moment we lose all supports and certainties, there awaits us an embrace of love that will not let us fall into emptiness.

Faith is converted into love—sometimes not until the last gate, sometimes earlier, perhaps. Where faith dies, love continues to burn, so darkness cannot have the final victory. Is it our love or His? It's a pointless question. There is only one love.

༉

Are we then to dread the age of secularism, atheism, and the "cooling of many people's faith," or can we perceive it as a mysterious contribution of historical time to the Easter drama, to the silence of Holy Saturday, when on the surface nothing is happening—when, as is the tradition in Czech churches, the tabernacles are open and empty on the altars and people kneel at "God's Tomb"—but somewhere "down below" a mighty struggle between life and death is taking place? Can we persevere in these moments and seek their meaning without immediately, at every "return of religion," all too hastily perceiving the radiance of the promised Easter morning?

I lived through a period in my country's fairly recent history when religion and the church were virtually eradicated from public life. State atheism, *civitas terrena,* the "secular city" seemed to have triumphed. I first encountered a living church when I was at the threshold of adulthood. I sensed that "something was happening" in some of the churches still, that they were not all simply museums, and that somewhere something still survived of the world of believers, the world of yesterday. It never occurred to me in the least that one day it might have some bearing on my world and my life. But it was precisely in those circumstances, at that period, in that world "without images," that my faith came into being.

I remember well the moment when, as a romantic eighteen-year-old who had just started reading the Bible (I had yet to find anyone to tell me how silly it is to read the Bible like a novel "from cover to cover"), I first wandered into a church—it was dilapidated and had a collapsed roof, like many of the churches in the Czech border areas at the time—in order to make up my mind as to whether I believed in God or not. And yes, that ramshackle church—a church totally devoid of images, one that lacked even an altar—was a place where God was able to speak to the seeker.

Of course, the ideas that led me to faith at that time did not simply fall out of the blue. There was the Bible that had been passed on from generation to generation. There were books written by Christians. There was evidence of faith in music, architecture, and painting, which only subsequently, of course, I was able gradually to decipher as "signs of faith." There were people who were not "churchgoers" as such, yet there was "something" present in their mentality and behavior, or in their memory or subconscious. When "the spark jumped," it gradually became clearer to me that all around us there was still a lot of Christianity left.

I had scarcely started to be curious and to peer out of my hiding place in the treetop when *Jesus passed by*—and He would patiently turn up over and over again in many forms until I eventually heard Him distinctly enough and realized that He was calling me by name.

Of course, there had to be a church here, so that I and many others like me could—in various ways—"chance upon" the treasure hidden in the field. It had to be here for all those centuries, and it had to have survived during periods of persecution—either, at the cost of compromise, on the fringe of society, or underground at the cost of great risk, including martyrdom. And my path also led from "intellectual conversion" toward flesh-and-blood Christians. Many of them had undergone conversions much more dramatic than mine and from a much greater distance, having had to complete their road to Damascus and discover Christians there like Paul did, no longer with hostility or hostile intentions, but with a readiness to learn and a yearning to be accepted.

I don't underestimate the church, therefore, even though my own conversion occurred mostly outside its visible walls rather than within "the family of the faith." Christian faith undoubtedly has a legitimate ecclesiastical dimension and is not a purely private matter. However, I do not intend to steer all dialogue about faith onto the topic of the church and certainly have no wish to discuss gossip about scandals in the church or speculation about church policies, let alone "the future of the church," for that matter. Whenever I see a church in decline somewhere—in whatever sense—I do not despair. After all, I personally have lived through a great deal, and Christians in the course of the twentieth century saw and lived through much more than I have.

I don't shrink from the holes left in the church roof by some tempest or other. I recall that it was through those gaping holes that I first glimpsed God's face.

CHAPTER 4

ॐ

Barefoot

God is mystery—that should be the first and last sentence of any theology. Whenever we write or say anything about God, each of our phrases should—just like the warriors of Israel who marched into battle preceded by singers—be accompanied by two angels crying (as is the practice in the liturgy of the East): Mystery! Mystery! On my writing desk in Prague there stands a large wooden angel that reminds me: if you write about God, remember that you are entering a cloud of enigma. Take care not to think for even a moment that you have gained sufficient insight into His mystery; the most you can hope for is to touch Him lightly from behind, like the hemorrhaging woman touched the hem of Jesus's cloak.

What can we say about God? First and last the words of the psalm: "Cloud and darkness surround him." Faith and atheism are two views of that reality—the hiddenness of God, His transcendence, and His impenetrable mystery; they are two possible interpretations of the same reality, seen from two opposite sides.

St. Thomas Aquinas declares that, while it is possible for us to be convinced intellectually of God's existence, we are obliged to add that we do not know *who* God is (what He is "in Himself") and *how*

He is, and what the verb "is" means when referring to God. That goes beyond all our experience, our entire imagination, and the scope of our reasoning; God is—as Anselm taught—greater than anything we can possibly conceive. God definitely *is not* in the sense that *we are,* or things *are,* or the world *is.* It is that radical difference between His existence and our existence in the world that provides scope for the existence of atheism and agnosticism—and also faith. If God were ordinary and "readily available," there would be no point in passionate faith, no courage of human hope to say "yes" in the face of the unfathomable, to say that "yes" in the face of everything that urges us to say a "no" of resignation, or at best a skeptical "maybe." That is precisely why the never-ending contest between belief and unbelief is so fascinating and dramatic.

Nevertheless the Bible is a book of paradoxes—almost every assertion is offset by some other assertion that is, or seems to be, its opposite, so that we are prevented from settling lazily on the surface of things or in the shallow slough of over-facile certainties. One of the Bible's paradoxes consists of two assertions that need to be treated with enormous caution, so that the one gently counterbalances the other: "God is an impenetrable mystery" (*He dwells in unapproachable light*)—but also: God and man are alike (*God created man in his own image*).

"God created man in his image; in the divine image he created him," we read on the first page of scripture. So God and man are alike in some way. Yet if we exaggerate this truth we end up with primitive anthropomorphic notions of God, and it is a short step from them to the atheists' opposite assertion that man created God in his own image!

God and man are "in some way" similar, nonetheless, and that is extremely important for us—including for our story of Zac-chaeus. God's image is not some abstract, ideal human being, the kind depicted in anatomy or ethics textbooks, the idea of man, "human nature," existing in the imagination of theologians but not in the real world and history. Every human being—you and I, Zacchaeus yesterday and today—is an image of God; *the infinity of God can be represented solely by the infinite plurality of the human world.* Each one of those portraits of God is completely different—but each one is signed by its author, every one is authentic, every one is true! Insofar as we preserve our *originality* imprinted and stored by God—and we do not become a copy of others: a *forgery*—each of us will proclaim through our unmistakable uniqueness something new and truthful about God and His inexhaustible mystery.

And so the question naturally arises: isn't Zacchaeus (and I'm sure we've realized that he is *our image,* and if not of all of us, at least many of us)—that hidden, yet watchful human being—also in some way a mirror, a likeness, a *picture of God*—i.e., *a hidden, yet watchful God?*

ᢢ

Since time immemorial, people—and particularly theologians—have yearned to peek into that cloud, to catch a glimpse of God *as He is in Himself.* Is this really out of the question? Is this sight really so totally and definitively inaccessible as St. Thomas believed? Or does God, who is "hidden yet watchful," allow Himself after all to be recognized more intimately in the course of and through histor-ical events than the scholastic theologians were capable of grasping? After all, He showed His face and passion, as well as the pain of His heart, several times in the history of the chosen nation (if we leave aside for later consideration how He is revealed in the life story of His only begotten son). Doesn't God reveal Himself in a very specific way at the present time, when many have the impression that He is *trying hard to make Himself scarce*? Do not those today who have not ceased seeking Him have a rare opportunity for new spiritual insight and understanding?

I spoke on one occasion[1] of the need to lay ourselves open more radically to the mystery of God, to "put into brackets" many familiar perceptions of God and find—like Paul on the Areopagus—"the altar to the unknown god." Immediately afterward, one of the participants sent me a short text by the contemporary French theologian Joseph Moingt, which expressed similar views to my own and inspired my further reflections on the subject.

Moingt boldly asks how God can be discovered "as He is in Himself": the only way that God can exist for us, in our language and in our world, is if we let Him exist as "our" God. However, He exists for Himself, and we have access to Him, to the way He is in Himself, only insofar as we are prepared to forgo attempts at making Him "our God," our property, God in our image, the custodian of our past, who is important to us as a confirmation of our common identity— insofar as we are prepared to let Him be "other" and exist for others.[2]

Invoking Jesus's words, "it is better for you that I go" (John 16:7), Moingt urges us to *let God go!* That is to say: Let Him go to others! Let us discover that He is not simply "the God of our fathers," our inherited property, but also the "God of others." Only then will we discover that He is the one universal God, and not a particular deity among the deities of the Chaldean Empire; precisely because He is the one universal God, He is not a God on which we could have a monopoly.

And we should not even be scared, says Moingt, if, in the interval between losing the "God of the fathers" and finding *the faith of the sons* (no longer an "inherited religion" but a free response to the way the Spirit blows today), atheism makes an appearance: This period of becoming empty, of exchanges with strangers, can be a period without God, but this time of absence is necessary, so that we enable God to offer Himself to us the way He is. We must let Him come in his newness, even if we might then be incapable of recognizing the God of our fathers in the one who comes from elsewhere.

Moingt's position is a radical emulation of St. Paul. The apostle presents Christianity to us as a faith capable of dissociating itself from its past, ridding itself of old customs and certainties, rejecting particularity *and going to others*. Paul presents Christianity to us not as an aspect of some orthodoxy or orthopraxis, but as a new *politeia*—a new way of communication between people and between societies. Paul's *crossing of the borders of Israel and setting out for the "peoples" (the pagans) should be a paradigm for the entire history of the church.*

This is what is specifically Christian! In like manner, the church should constantly come out from its Christian past and have the capacity to leave much of its "heritage" boldly behind it. This was and still is its task. But when we look at history, we get a different picture. The church quickly withdrew into a new particularism of its own; the notion of a "new Israel" did not engender the courage to be constantly *people on the way*, boldly crossing all borders. Instead, we tended to become a "second Israel," another particular community *alongside* Israel, rather than a truly *new* Israel that would take up the dynamic aspect of the chosen people's faith—Abraham's departure from his homeland and the Exodus, the departure from Egypt, above all Paul's crossing the frontiers of the Mosaic Law, the fron-

tiers of Judaism, *in search of all human beings without any difference.*
The church became more of a new particular group among others;
it started to guard its frontiers and turn its faith into a "heritage of
the fathers," inherited property. The *hellenization* of Christianity,
Moingt maintains, which enabled the early church to leave the
rather narrow context of a single nation and enter the much wider
cultural context of the then world, paradoxically led to a new
"Judaization" of Christianity and a fixation once more on "one language." Yet the church should pentecostally "speak all languages,"
and not presuppose that our Christianity is the language whereby
God speaks to all and that everyone is required to understand it. It
is we who must try to understand others; only in that way can we
then try to address others intelligibly.

His use of this term → is unfortunate because I think it detracts from the point he is trying to make.

Moingt repeats again and again: let us give up the "God of the
fathers" and find the Father of Jesus Christ; let us have the courage
to leave behind "inherited religion" and our infantile fixation on the
forms of the past in favor of *the faith of the sons*—with everything that
Jesus says about the freedom of those who are not slaves, but sons,
friends, and partners. Paul had the courage to reject all previous
"certainties" and the "quiescence of compromise" as a temptation—
a temptation to seek salvation elsewhere than in the reconciliation of
God with the world through the blood of Christ's cross. We must
not make light of the Gospel's novelty by clinging to the past and remaining in the narrow confines of earlier traditions; we must not
empty the cross of Christ that became a bridge of reconciliation and destroyed previous barriers.

He means "The God of the religiously narrow minded—the Jewish zealots" of Paul's day.

The appeal to abandon the God of the fathers and replace Him
with the Father of Jesus Christ can, at first sight, recall one of the
oldest (and most dangerous) heresies: Marcion's attempt to set

Here is the correction!

against each other the God of the Old Testament and the Father of Jesus Christ. In the face of that heresy, the early church realized the risk of deracination and shallowness if the "memory of Israel" were renounced, and so it established the Canon of Holy Scripture, which incorporated from then on the Hebrew Bible and constructed its new theology around a radically new interpretation of Jewish tradition and the mutual compatibility of the two *Testaments*. However, Moingt does not contend that the "God of the fathers" is a false god; indeed, he categorically rules out such an interpretation and does not in any way identify this "God of the fathers" with the God of the Hebrew Bible—he is certainly not calling for a "clearance sale" of Christian tradition. His concern is to *break with the concept of God as "property,"* which we have inherited as some kind of chattel that can be handled and to which we can lay a special claim. The discovery of one living God (who is also, of course, "the God of our fathers") resides in the discovery that He is also the God *of others.* It does not mean giving up our own tradition, but simply not being fixated with it and instead exposing ourselves to the adventure of discovering it in a wider context—and, by engaging in dialogue with others, learning to look at it "with others' eyes" also.

In this sense I realize that the radical Paulinism of Joseph Moingt is the very same message as the one at the center of our reflections on Zacchaeus—simply said in other words and viewed from a slightly different perspective. Let us not leave God solely to the "religiously assured"! God is *always greater, semper maior,* as Ignatian mysticism teaches us. No one has a monopoly on Him. "Our" God is also the God of *others*—including seekers and those who don't know Him. Yes, God is *above all* the God of seekers, of people on the journey.

If we profess the God of Abraham—and not some abstract philosophical concept of a vague "supreme being" who might appeal to everybody—we prove our faithfulness, not by clinging to a specific tradition of the past, but, like Abraham, by entering new territory. "Our" God is a pilgrim God, the God of the eternal exodus, who leads us out of the homes and homelands even though we would prefer to settle in them and fortify them—and also enclose Him in our borders, in the confines of our notions, concepts, traditions, and creeds.

God remains a radical mystery, which is precisely why attempts to "manipulate" God are so ludicrous as well as blasphemous. Yet God is not only hidden, He is also *watchful*—He reveals Himself and sees those who seek Him, as scripture says about divine wisdom.

God is on watch for those who are on watch for Him—and perhaps we could add: *our watchfulness,* our spiritual experience and the spiritual experience of others, are in a way *His* watchfulness, the way He is among us. *He is in our openness.* Rather than our "counterpart," He is our *foundation,* the fount not only of our existence but also of what our existence achieves. He is therefore also the foundation and fount of our seeking, our watchfulness, our openness, our self-transcendence. In that sense are we most "similar" to God, who constantly transcends Himself and pours Himself out in love. He "pours Himself out" not only *into* our seeking; He is not in it simply as a *thing* we could look for—certainly we could never find Him among the "things" and objective existences. God is present in *our very seeking*—and He is present in the world also through our seeking. When we address our prayers to "heaven," what we are saying is that God's mystery is not confined within frontiers that are attainable by us. Nevertheless, there is no need to seek Him "in heaven"—He is already genuinely present on earth in those very prayers, as Paul himself teaches us: when we pray, the spirit of God intercedes for us with inexpressible groanings.[3] God is in our prayer, our yearning, our seeking, in our very questions.

God is in this world and in our language (and our language is the most important and most intrinsic structure of the human world—it is a prism through which we see the world), by virtue of the fact that we allow Him to exist as our God. Moingt's idea, mentioned earlier, does not entail reducing God to "something merely human"; it is simply consistent Incarnation theology taken to its consequences. And I have a similar take on his phrase about "God, as He is in Himself," to whom we give scope by not limiting Him as our own God, by not fettering the concept of God with our own monopolistic claims, by "allowing Him" to be the God of others also. It is in the "mirror of Easter," in the revelation of God's most inner mystery through Christ (which we have deliberately not yet spoken about and which will be treated later), that we see God's transcendence, God's openness to others—in Jesus, in His *relationship to "others,"* in His radical love without boundaries, which eventually takes Him to the cross and reveals itself fully at that very point. And Jesus's love and openness toward others, *which is the most radical revelation of God,* is to find a continuation in us, in our attitudes to others, to people who are different from us. Jesus challenged us to "to do the works that I do" and "to do greater ones than these" (John 14:12).

And therefore we can follow on from Moingt and say that our openness toward others is our openness toward God, because through Christ, God shows solidarity with *others*—and our openness toward God and our neighbors *is* God's openness toward us and the world, because through Christ (through the mystery of the Incarnation) God shows solidarity with us and seeks to be present in the world through our testimony of love. As Meister Eckhart maintained, the eye by which we see God and the eye by which God sees us *is the selfsame eye.*

༄

I would like to return to one sentence in Moingt's short text. When he remarks that Paul endowed the church with a paradigm shift in its relationship with others and strangers, giving it the courage to abandon its own past, he says that we ought not to wait until the others sit down at our table, but that we should have *the courage to sit down at theirs.* He thus employs—probably unintentionally—the same expression that Thérèse de Lisieux used when, on the brink of death, she felt *solidarity with unbelievers*: Christ sat her down at their table and gave her their bread to eat with them.

It is not entirely clear from the short text of Moingt's I have at my disposal what "others" he had in mind; it would seem that his gaze was fixed above all on the non-European cultures and the "poor nations," to whom we cannot take "the God of our fathers" or our traditional religious notions, which are strongly marked by all the limits of our particular Western tradition. Nevertheless, it is certainly possible to extend his appeal—however he himself intended it—to other "others," to devotees of other religions, as well as to "nonbelievers," doubters, seekers, and "those who believe in another way."

The Second Vatican Council in the early 1960s was a grandiose attempt by the Catholic Church to draw closer to the modern world and thereby make Christ and His message clearer and more approachable for modern people. It was that Council, which set itself the task of bridging the gulf between the church and "the rest," that inaugurated a dialogue with modern secular culture and secular humanism, the other Christian churches, and believers of non-Christian religions, as well as with agnostics and atheists. What was new and specific to that Council was above all the fact that, unlike almost every previous Council, it did not exhort the church to heal the world—by consolidation of faith, fervency of devotion, piety, and moral reform—but instead came up with a different diagnosis and hence also a new therapy. The church was above all to *demonstrate solidarity with people of the present day*, with the modern world and with its problems. "The joys and the hopes, the grief, and the anxieties of the men of this age, especially those who are poor or in any way afflicted, these are the joys and hopes, the grief and anxieties of the followers of Christ," states the momentous celebratory opening sentence of the Council's most important document.[4]

After almost half a century it is necessary to ask to what extent the church has fulfilled this marriage vow of love, honor, and fidelity to present-day people, to what extent *the bride of Christ* has recognized Christ in contemporary humanity, especially in those of its members who are suffering or poor, but also in those who seek and thirst for meaning, not to mention those who eat the *bitter bread* of separation from God.

The post-Council enthusiasts bore aloft standards inscribed with two words above all: "dialogue" and "aggiornamento." Aggiornamento—"bringing up to date," that favorite and still-quoted word of John XXIII, doesn't mean and was never intended to mean a superficial modernization in the sense of the "conforming to the spirit of this world" that scripture rightly warns us against. "Aggiornamento" in Italian means simply updating, such as when we decide to revise, after ten years, the list of people invited to our birthday celebration and discover that some of the names need deleting: this person has died, this one has moved away, and this one I've fallen out with, but that interesting couple I met on holiday last year doesn't figure on the list yet. The Council's "aggiornamento" was intended as a revision of issues that the church should emphasize and an updating of the means available to do so.

In one of his parables, Jesus calls for just such a revision: he speaks about the builder who must carefully think whether he has enough materials before he sets about building a tower, lest he become a target of mockery, and also about the king setting out for battle who first ought to count his forces, and if they are insufficient should seek a truce instead. Aggiornamento was certainly not intended to mean a hasty "truce with the modern world," which the church could quickly conclude when it fairly realistically discovered that the battle it had been waging against modernity no longer had any prospects of a triumphant victory. Unfortunately, some enthusiastic supporters of postconciliar reforms really did interpret "aggiornamento" in that superficial way, and in so doing they provoked even greater distrust of and resistance to those reforms within the traditionalist camp. Incidentally, Jesus's parable about the builder and the king—i.e., about men who ought to behave *rationally*—surprisingly concludes with an appeal for rationality of quite the opposite kind: the paradoxical wisdom of the kingdom of God according to which *loss is gain*: the one who does not renounce all his possessions cannot be my disciple.[5] Perhaps if they were to reflect on the implications of that parable, many people in the church might find they had no need to be alarmed about the "losses" that the church suffered following the Council, contrary to the expectations of the majority. Some losses—as Jesus teaches us—are gains. Many crises—said C. G. Jung—are opportunities.

I can't help thinking that the world and the church would look very different if there were more people willing to view the Council's call for solidarity with this world (including the world of the "unbelievers," those who are most radically "other" and different), not as a cue to superficially modernize the rhetoric and external resources of "evangelization," but as a profound awareness *of God's hiddenness, of how He "reveals" Himself through the experience of "unbelievers,"* as we were taught by Thérèse de Lisieux on her deathbed. Thérèse could only indicate the path—which is what any good teacher does in any case—and bequeath to us the task of thinking through and accomplishing the spiritual journey.

Could not something of that kind invest the postconciliar development of Catholic Christianity—and Christianity in general, of course, because it is foolish by now to think about Christianity solely in terms of single traditions and to fail to see how sparks naturally leap across denominational boundaries, how churches influence each other for good or ill—with a greater depth, and thereby fulfill in a more practical and consistent manner what was promised in the aforementioned preface to the *Gaudium et Spes* constitution?

✣

Of course, some steps have been taken. The great pope of the Council, Paul VI—whose texts (if we disregard the occasional neo-Baroque trimmings of the "Vatican dialect") sometimes contain

very remarkable and bold ideas—declared that God Himself speaks
to the church of our day also through the lack of faith of many of
our neighbors. We find similar themes, developed chiefly by the
French "new theology" of the first half of the twentieth century, in
several of the Council's documents. Whereas, at the time of the
First Vatican Council, atheism was perceived either as an intellectual error—which had to be vanquished by means of apologetics
with metaphysical proofs—or as a sin through lack of goodwill, the
Second Vatican Council considered the main cause of atheism to
be insufficiently credible witness on the part of the church. It also
distinguished between the various types of atheism and took a differentiated view of its causes and significance, and of how and in
what sense they are a challenge to faith. The teaching of Karl
Rahner—who was once one of the Council's most influential
theological advisers—about "anonymous Christians" (as well as the
Rahner-inspired texts about "anonymous catechumens" by the
Rome-based Czech theologian Vladimír Boublík), which may
seem outdated by now, nevertheless represented a positive step in
the direction not only of believers of other religions, but also of
nonbelievers, semibelievers, or people of other beliefs in the secular world.

It is not fortuitous that the "worker-priests" in France chose
"little Thérèse" as their patron saint and symbolically chose Lisieux
as the location of their seminary. They had abandoned the familiar
structures of church government and the traditional style of clerical
presence in society in favor of factories and civilian professions, in
order to make their own the hopes and anxieties of the labor world.
(Inspired by that experiment, Teilhard de Chardin once wrote that
the modern world of science and research was also in urgent need

of its "worker-priests"—words that were to have a fundamental influence on my own life and vocation.)

During forty years of Communist rule in our country—exactly the number of years that Israel needed to escape from Egyptian slavery into the land of freedom[6]—hundreds of priests worked in civilian employment. They included those from whom the Communist authorities had removed "state permission to discharge priestly duties" or to whom that permission (without which any manifestation of their religion could be qualified as a criminal act and punished) had not been restored after their release from prison, concentration camp, or forced service in "labor units" of the army, as well as those who had never had any chance of receiving such permission because of their "political unreliability" and were prepared for ordination and secretly ordained for the "underground church," as was my case. That experience of priests in civilian employment, which remarkably parallels the pastoral experiments of "worker-priests" in Western Europe and Latin America, was the result of political coercion. Nonetheless, it was accepted by some of us not simply as an imposition from outside, but also as a specific vocation and opportunity, as a challenge.

Whereas the confrontation with Nazism gave rise to the remarkable Christian and Jewish "post-Auschwitz theology," the confrontation with "third world" poverty led to Latin American liberation theology, and the confrontation with Western secular society led to "secularization theology" and "death of God theology," the experience of the confrontation with Communism and the "anonymous" presence of priests in a world from which religion had been systematically displaced *has yet to be the subject of adequate theological reflection and cultivation*. Of course, the experience of the confrontation with Communism strongly influenced the pontificate of John Paul II, not only in terms of his emphasis on human rights and European unification, but also, for instance, in his concern for the penitential cleansing of the church's historical memory and "healing the wounds of the past"; this was a response not simply to the Gospel's call for repentance and "change of heart," but also to constant criticism from those who rejected the church and Christianity in general precisely because of those historical burdens. However, I have something else in mind, something that usually only comes into existence when the church is truly brought to its knees (which never completely happened in Poland, for instance, thanks to the strong links between Catholicism and Polish national identity), where one is obliged to ask the radical question whether a moment came when the church—or at least the church in its previous historical form—*passed away,* and what it can bequeath of its experiences to those who may one day be inspired by them once more.[7]

Yes, I'm profoundly convinced that, precisely in circumstances where the church was crushed and trampled into the dust like a seed, that seed ought to bring forth fruit at last. It doesn't look as though the fruit will be an outwardly flourishing church, if by that we envisage full churches and seminaries, nor need it necessarily be a clear flame of new theological thinking. Maybe what can and should emerge is a new boldness to approach those "others." This could help achieve what I am convinced our entire Euro-Atlantic civilization—which is "post-Christian" and "postsecular" at one and the same time—sorely needs.

Perhaps in the face of aggressive forms of *Islamism,* which are an attempt to use religion for political ends, there will ensue not simply a "counterreaction" in the form of aggressive radical secularism or the reinforcement of Christian fundamentalism, but also a *new sincerity,* a new maturity—a new type of "faith/nonfaith" dialogue that would allow what is spiritually vigorous in the world of faith (perhaps merely in the form of a longing for profound change or a new exodus) to encounter anew what is vigorous (perhaps simply in the form of spiritual restlessness and thirst) in the world beyond the traditional boundaries of "religion."

ॐ

The country I was born in and where I live is regarded as one of the "most atheistic nations on earth." But is it possible to measure belief solely according to the number of those who acknowledge membership in churches, attend church, or answer in the affirmative when asked by pollsters if they consider themselves to be believers—and regard the rest automatically as atheists? How would we take into account all the "Zacchaeuses"?

I once coined the expression "timid piety" to describe a relationship to religion that is fairly widespread among Czechs. In one of his books, the Czech Catholic writer Jaroslav Durych describes his visit to Spain just prior to World War II and compares Spanish and Czech styles of piety. He saw Spaniards praying in front of Baroque crucifixes with arms dramatically outstretched in the shape of a cross, and he recalled that Czech expressions of piety are much more restrained, plain, and discreet, if not timid, as if the Czech Catholics were somehow still aware of the gaze of skeptics or nonbelievers on them. Yes, and maybe there was a skeptic deep down in each of them; maybe that skeptic "inside" distanced them from many manifestations of church piety. But does it necessarily distance them from God? The expression "timid piety" denotes not only the style of piety of some Christians, but also the reserved attitude of a large part of the population in the Czech lands (and particularly influential and educated sections of society) toward ecclesiastical forms of Christianity. But we should not confuse that reserved attitude with atheism. In the case of many, it is something that could be described, using Karl Rahner's term, as "anonymous Christianity," or it could be the reserved religious attitude dealt with in this book in relation to the figure of Zacchaeus. The reasons for that detachment are clearly deeply rooted in the religious history of our country.

After the upheavals and crises caused by the Hussite revolution and its subsequent religious divisions, Catholicism returned in triumph to my country chiefly during the Thirty Years' War, in the wake of the victorious Habsburg troops. The old confession was replanted by means of enthusiastic missionaries, the educational activity of the Jesuits, and the allure of Baroque culture, but also by violence, oppression, and the merciless banishment of those who refused to subscribe to the faith of the victors. Yet a victory involving the violent suppression of the enemy and his culture tends to be Pyrrhic. What is "repressed and displaced," what isn't processed and integrated, often returns in different forms. Sigmund Freud convinced us of this principle in respect to individuals' lives, and his nonconformist pupil Carl Gustav Jung suggested a similar mechanism with regard to cultural conflict.

When confronting the paganism of antiquity, the early church managed to absorb, creatively process, and integrate many treasures of ancient Greece and Rome, and subsequently it proved capable of drawing on many elements of Celtic and Slavonic cultures. On the eve of the modern age, Jesuit missionaries demonstrated great sensibility for the values of Chinese and Japanese cultures. Wherever, on the threshold of modern times, the Baroque "Catholic Reformation," with its great saints, mystics, organizers, thinkers, and artists, evolved in parallel with the spiritual currents of the Renaissance and Protestant Reformation (and often in creative and dynamic tension with them), religious life acquired a new vim and vitality. On the other hand, in those places where, after the Council of Trent, Catholicism tended to assume the form of "Counter-Reformation"—a counterculture vis-à-vis the above-mentioned spiritual currents—something was introduced into the foundation of triumphant Catholicism that in later times was to emerge as a dangerous explosive or a noxious blight. Whereas in France the Great Revolution abolished the old order, in the countries under Habsburg rule the worm of formalism, externality, and hypocrisy quietly and unobtrusively eroded the edifice of the old faith. There was often no room within the church for national revivalist sentiment—and as a result, many who took their faith very seriously found themselves in time "on the other shore."[8] Others did not publicly display their dissatisfaction with shallow religiosity and did not particularly concern themselves with it; however, in some of those cases, a fateful crossroads was reached, and their own spiritual life (in the broadest sense of the word) slowly and gradually, but ever more obviously, parted ways with what the church's piety offered and stood for. People grew accustomed to seeking answers to their basic questions of existence elsewhere than beneath the pulpit. Jesus, in the form He was presented and interpreted by many of those who claimed to speak in His name, ceased to speak to the seekers of those days.

When I reflect on the Czech culture of the past two centuries,

I find that what is most lively and interesting exists beyond the traditional, official, and institutional ambit of the church. It is possible—particularly among the poets—to find individuals with a considerable spiritual sensibility, but even that tends to have only a tenuous connection with a classical religious tradition. Many cultural figures have displayed a frantic defiance of all "official" and institutional forms of religion, although this is more anticlericalism than atheism and often indicates a strange love-hate relationship (occasionally hatred born out of frustrated love) for which German has the apt expression *Hassliebe*. When I mentally scan a portrait gallery of the key figures of Czech culture in the nineteenth and twentieth centuries (including the two "philosopher presidents," Tomáš Masaryk and Václav Havel), I must aver that none of them was an "atheist"; each of them was in some way extremely open to the "transcendental dimension of life"—and especially to its ethical consequences. Nevertheless, none of them was willing to speak about the transcendental in the traditional language of the church.

It was not only due to the Communist persecution of religion and the decades of the forcibly imposed state ideology—"scientific atheism"—that the word "God" disappeared from the list of most frequently used words in the Czech language. When I hear Václav Havel speak, not about God, but about "the horizon of horizons" and "something or someone above us," this is not just vague religiosity of the kind ironically described as "somethingism" (i.e., the most widespread religion of our day, whose credo is "I may not believe in God, but there must be *something* above us"), nor is it "religious dilettantism," as the Czech Protestant theologian Josef L. Hromádka dubbed the phenomenon.

I have a sense that in this "timid piety" that eschews many

forms of the church, including traditional religious language, *Zacchaeus lives once again,* and is still avoiding the crowds. On various occasions I have uttered very bitter and critical words about the religious indifference and "religious illiteracy" of the society of which I am part. But I am still of the belief that these phenomena are only superficial, that deep down the situation can be and certainly is different.

I recall that, during a flight from Rome to Madrid, I once got into conversation with my neighbor, an American, who was a veteran of World War II and had spent many years as a journalist in Rome. He had just retired and was looking for a place to spend the rest of his life. He talked to me about an Italian priest, a Vatican diplomat in America, and said of him: "That man managed to get his way into places that almost nobody who wasn't born in America or hadn't spent the most of his life there would ever have had access to. You know, when most people look at Americans all they see is our noisiness, our back-slapping joviality, our stereotypical broad smiles and empty chitchat at parties. But that's only our mask, the surface, a rampart that we don't let many people cross. That priest didn't let himself be taken in; he got beneath the surface and came to understand the *thirteenth chamber of the American soul.*"

Many years ago, still at the time of the Soviet Union, I watched a film by the director Andrei Tarkovsky in the company of a connoisseur of Russian literature. That colleague leaned over to me and whispered: "You see—wherever you dig a bit below the surface in the Russian nation you come across religion." Maybe all nations have their "thirteenth chamber" of the soul, even our "atheist" one.

How can Christians, churches, and theologians approach those Zacchaeuses, how can they reach the "thirteenth chamber" of our nation's soul and the soul of our culture? That was the question put to me by telephone during a radio discussion in which I had touched on those themes in passing. The hand on the studio clock relentlessly indicated the imminent end of the program, and so there was no time for any lengthy explanation. "Barefooted," I replied. And in one sentence I referred to the legend of St. Adalbert, who, before he ascended his bishop's throne in Prague in the middle of the ninth century, is reputed to have removed his shoes in front of the cathedral as a sign of humility and then approached the altar in bare feet.

I think that Adalbert's gesture can serve as an important example for our epoch, and certainly for the church in the Czech lands. And it does not concern in the first place the frequently discussed issue of church property and the purely external displays of repellent triumphalism; I do not underestimate these things, but they are, after all, secondary. The poverty and humility that we should display in these times relate to much deeper and more fundamental matters.

Boldly reaching out to others in the footsteps of the apostle Paul, entering the "thirteenth chamber" of people's hearts and the hearts of cultures, entering the cloud of God's mystery—these are all in fact just one path, and that path can only be taken *in bare feet.* Like Moses before the burning bush, we are called on to remove our sandals, because *the place where we stand*—although we never suspected it—*is holy ground.*[9]

ↄ

The Dispute about the Beauty of
Dulcinea del Toboso

It's possible that my understanding for people who "don't go to church" partly stems from the fact that ever since I became a priest—or rather, since I emerged from "the underground," from "illegality," and was given the job of founding and running a very specific parish in Prague—I don't attend church very often (except of course my own). I scarcely ever hear any sermons apart from my own, which for that reason I have had a surfeit of and find it hard to listen to them again at all. But that is one of the crosses a priest must bear: "Priesterleben—Opferleben"—a priest's life is a life of sacrifice—a German colleague of mine is wont to say (usually after a heavy Sunday lunch).

But I did recently hear a sermon by one of my colleagues; its theme was "Mary, image of the church." The idea that Jesus's mother is an icon of the church, which was so cherished by John Paul II, is not foreign to me, particularly if we develop this metaphor in the spirit of the Eastern church and its theology of icons. However, the sermon was so sweetly sentimental, superficial, and without sparkle that I was provoked to suggest another metaphor to the preacher afterward: the church as Dulcinea del Toboso.

If we perceive it theologically, not simply sociologically—mystically, not simply bureaucratically—the church is a mystery for us: above all we do not know its boundaries, we don't even know where it begins and where it ends, who belongs to it and who doesn't. St. Augustine wrote that many who think they are inside are outside, but also vice versa. The last Council stressed that the church is a sacrament, i.e., it is a symbol and also an instrument of the unity of all people and nations in Christ, a unity of humankind that cannot be entirely achieved within history, but is an "eschatological aspiration." Every human being—via the mystery of the Incarnation—is already linked "in some way" with the church. By virtue of their humanity, people are linked with Christ's humanity and therefore have a certain participation in His "mystical body" on earth. By and large, what people have in mind nowadays when they discuss the church and its problems is only the outward part—I'd almost say a shadow—of the mysterious dwelling of the resurrected Christ in the history of human society and His transformational impact upon it. Nevertheless, even a shadow is a manifestation of the real ("physical") presence of the church in history.

The fact that we can hear and read so many different things about the church of the past and the present, and that our individual personal experiences of it can be diametrically opposed—particularly when we encounter it in various parts of the world and in varied cultural contexts—should not surprise, puzzle, or irritate us. The church was, is, and will be multifaceted, and the experience of its multifariousness should shield us from the temptation to form a preconceived (and therefore necessarily limited, oversimplified, and superficial) notion of it.

That is to say, we don't really know what the church is like in reality, what it really looks like—just like Dulcinea del Toboso. Is she the grimy, coarse maid-of-all-work that Sancho Panza sees, or the noble lady that Don Quixote worships in her?

Authorities on Cervantes's work long ago drew attention to the brilliant dialectics of the celebrated novel. We have naturally been long under the impression that Sancho Panza, the genial realist, is right, while the Don is a dreamer and a pitiable crackpot. But a closer reading of the text shows that this might not be the case. There are things that Sancho quite simply does not see from his point of view. In short, Don Quixote and Sancho Panza are two aspects of the human being, two different perspectives on the world. Quixote is a featherbrain only without Sancho, while Sancho without Quixote is a philistine oaf. Neither the Don nor Sancho sees the real and complete Dulcinea; or, alternatively, both of them are right: Sancho is certainly correct as far as her outward appearance is concerned, while Quixote may perceive what is hidden within Dulcinea, her latent self; not what she visibly is, but what she could be—and maybe what she eventually will be.

My father once told me a story about one of his Jewish colleagues, who was asked at a party by someone—who was probably already well in his cups—"Mr. Silberstein, how come someone as debonair as you should have married such an ugly woman?" The old gentleman did not allow this impertinence to ruffle his composure: "Young man, if you had my eyes, she'd be the most beautiful woman in the world for you as well!" Yes, I admit that there are places and periods in the history of our church when we must really be madly in love and appear to some like crackpot knights when we want to talk about its beauty.

When we read the things that today's Sancho Panzas write

about the church in the tabloid press, we cannot doubt that there is some truth in them, but they are not the entire and complete truth. When we contemplate the church in the manner of mystics, as an apocalyptic bride descending from on high without spot or blemish, as the lovely maiden from the Song of Solomon and the Immaculate Virgin, we cannot doubt the legitimacy of that point of view either. But let us not close our ears when Sancho Panza comes knocking once more on the closed door of our meditative chamber in order to call us back down to earth with his perceptive remarks. The whole truth about the church does not reside either down on the ground or up in the mystical heights, nor "somewhere in between." There are not two or even three Dulcineas, just one single Dulcinea viewed from different perspectives.

Perception of the church evolves in time; the church reveals itself through its various facets both to the paparazzi of the tabloid press and to the theologians and mystics (albeit not to the same degree, of course), but we will not see its true face until that moment, described in the closing words of the Bible, of the arrival of the heavenly Jerusalem. We would not form a picture of Dulcinea (or the church) by comparing the descriptions or portraits produced by Don Quixote and Sancho Panza and then using a computer to create a perfect synthesis. The truth about Dulcinea is not the average of two contrary perspectives—it's not that easy. Perhaps the only point in placing these two different descriptions side by side is to challenge the monopoly of either individual and hence a partial viewpoint. Both the church and Dulcinea—like every woman, dare I add—are a mystery.

The literary historian Václav Černý wrote about the Good Soldier Švejk—one of the archetypal figures of Czech literature—that he was Sancho Panza without Don Quixote. That novel by Jaroslav Hašek, which has probably done more than any other book to spread the fame of Czech literature beyond the national frontiers, contains probably one of the most sarcastic descriptions of a religious service in world literature (including a sermon by a completely drunk field curate). It is a mass (and a church) seen through the eyes of Sancho Panza. There is definitely something authentic about that vision, and not simply because during World War I the Austrian army was bound to have had more than one drunken field curate; in hindsight, the whole of Europe at that period appears to us paralyzed with drunkenness.

During the same period, on the opposite side of the same battlefront, the "field curate" Teilhard de Chardin was penning texts that describe the bloody cataclysm of war as a mystic component of a "cosmic mass," as the mystery of the world's transformation process, out of which a new unity of humankind would be born. Who was right? Which of them is vindicated by today's reality? Is the answer to be found by weighing the number of drunken curates in today's wars on the one hand, and the extent of "new consciousness" among the present generation on the other?

The dispute between today's Don Quixotes and Sancho Panzas is still undecided and will probably continue to the end of the world. Or will "the two of them" manage to travel together through the world and act as mutual correctives, like the two heroes of Cervantes's novel? Can we learn from their disputes and differences, as well as from their compatibilities, to overcome our own temptations for one-sidedness? Will we be more patient and aware of the mysteries that are both revealed and concealed in the paradoxes at the heart of our world?

My constant endeavor to seek truth in contradictions, to resist interpretations that lay claim to a monopoly over truth while being unaware of their inevitable narrowness, is not relativism, which is so popular nowadays; it doesn't end with a sigh of resignation that "all truths are valid" or that truth is simply a matter of convention. I try to show my students the history of thought as movement, which is, however, not unidirectional and irreversible "progress," but rather the constant movement of a ball between two players standing on either side of a sports field. I encourage them not to fall prey to bias in favor of one or the other of the players, and also not to fix their eyes on the movement of the ball, because the decisive moment of insight is always that point in time when we realize that an infinite blue sky of mystery arches over the field of all our games and contests.

The fact that, on our human playing fields, we encounter truth always "in movement"—and often in the plural—should not tempt us to indulge in facile relativism and an attitude of resignation or skepticism toward Truth. The biosphere of Truth is mystery, inaccessible depths, and unreachable heights. Its homeland is the eschaton, the absolute future beyond the horizon of history—and its major role in the present is to be constantly in a state of opposition to our attempts to make absolutes out of some of our human attitudes, approaches, and opinions, which are limited by our own individual (not universal) experience. Not even our faith can pull Truth in its eschatological fullness down "from heaven to earth," nor build a tower that would reach up to heaven. Rather, it teaches us hope and perseverance in overcoming the temptation of resignation, skepticism, and triumphalism—teaches us to listen with an open and humble heart when Truth itself visits us and speaks to us—

even were it to go on speaking only "in a mirror and in riddles" and in ambiguous "signs of the times."

⁊

But let us return to the theme of the church and the mysterious Dulcinea. Many present-day Zacchaeuses do not feel distant from God or Christ, so much as distant from the church. When, a few years ago, I started a course at New York University entitled "Religion, Politics, and Culture in Central Europe" and I tried to discover what *Vorverständnis,* or preliminary understanding, of religion my students had, they would ask me: "Do you mean organized religion?"

Many people in today's Western world—including those who don't consider themselves at all to be "unmusical" in religious terms—have major reservations about "organized religion." When he was still Professor Ratzinger, Pope Benedict XVI strove to convince his readers that all professing Christians should be prepared to "put up with the discomfort of Christ's family." Some contemporary authors of spiritual literature place a similar emphasis. Ronald Rolheiser warns that faith divorced from the life of a specific historical church community can rapidly slip into the realm of personal fantasy and projections of our own desires. "Away from actual, historical community, whatever its faults, we have an open field to live an unchallenged life, to make religion a private fantasy that we can selectively share with a few like-minded individuals who will never confront us where we most need challenge. The churches are compromised, dirty and sinful, but, just like our blood families, they are also real. In the presence of people who share life with us regularly, we cannot lie, especially to ourselves, and delude ourselves into thinking we are generous and noble. In community the truth emerges and fantasies are dispelled."[1] In Rolheiser's view, standoffishness toward the church on account of its faults is often merely an excuse and a rationalization: in reality, people want to preserve their illusions about themselves but sense that in the church—just as in the family—they might lose them. Rolheiser includes in his analysis a very useful list of the common false expectations that people often associate with the church and that inevitably lead to frustrations and disappointments: the church cannot offer either a substitute for family intimacy, or a tight-knit club of like-minded people, or an elite of saints, etc.

I too consider our culture's frequent tendency to make the church the culprit and main cause of our problems in religious life to be a facile and shortsighted excuse, much like the trend to blame parents, society, etc., for all the faults and problems of the young. What Charles Sykes wrote about America being a "nation of victims"[2]—with everyone seeking the cause of problems anywhere else but in themselves: in others and external circumstance—applies just as much, if not more, to present-day Europe, and is certainly reflected in attitudes toward the church.

The loss of illusions about the church, which sooner or later happens to many enthusiastic converts, can also be a very useful and possibly inevitable test of the maturity of one's belief, in the same way that in the course of adolescence—at the latest—one has to endure a loss of illusions about one's parents' own perfection. In our relations with our parents, the collapse of these infantile projections is often associated with a painful crisis and a phase of aversion. Nevertheless, one ought sooner or later to achieve a new and more mature, loving relationship with one's parents. We should not draw the destructive conclusion from the discovery of our parents' imperfections and failings that the principles that they handed on to us, even when they turn out to be incapable themselves of living up to them in all situations, no longer apply and are no longer binding. I feel that both the "conservatives" who, at the moment of crisis, cling for dear life to the "mother church" and indignantly refuse to take into account its faults, and the "progressives," whose angry hypercritical approach sometimes tends to betray an uncontrolled "Oedipus complex" in their relationship to the church authorities, demonstrate in two symmetrical ways a failure to cope with that test of maturity.

I have virtually ceased paying any attention to these polemics between "conservatives" and "progressives." I have learned to live with my church ("love bears all things"). When I once read St. Paul's letter during a celebration of a golden wedding anniversary and imagined what the couple must have gone through during their half a century of marriage, it struck me that our life in and with the church also calls perforce for quite a lot of patient fidelity, generosity, humor, and tolerance. Ought an aging priest let himself be put to shame by that elderly man and wife?

I have hinted several times that I don't find the subject of current inner church disputes—the things about the church that usually interest the media—to be of any great importance, yet I'm not irritated in the least when Zacchaeuses adopt and maintain a reserved attitude to those aspects of the church. It doesn't worry me if they have a somewhat "less committed" attitude toward the institutional form of the church. This does not mean, however, that my ideal is some "nonecclesiastical Christianity"—unreal, unspecific, unattached to history or society—let alone some hazy, esoteric, New Age–style religiosity.

I feel concern for the Zacchaeuses, for the church, and for the society that the church and the Zacchaeuses inhabit—in equal measure. I feel a responsibility to ensure that "individual seekers" of the Zacchaeus type are not manipulated by anyone to conform to a present notion of "standard believers," and that they are not driven out of the ambit of the church—that they are, quite simply, accorded freedom to determine how close they want to be to the visible forms of today's church-based Christianity.

I'm afraid that many priests—in our country, at least—have learned certain techniques for transforming interested persons and sympathizers into orderly, rank-and-file members of the church and feel they have failed if in some cases none of their techniques "worked." But that would mean that many of their encounters with the Zacchaeuses of today and tomorrow will cause them bitter disappointment—and I would like to spare them that (both parties, in fact). We have to learn to create space for the Zacchaeuses, including those who will never become "standard parishioners," or at least to respect the space that they create around themselves.

Yes, generally speaking—and particularly if our churches will appear in the future more or less the way they do now (and as far as I know, God has promised us no miracle in that respect)—the Zacchaeuses will occupy a place on the fringe of the visible church. And that place on the fringe is extremely important, not only for the Zacchaeuses but also for the church! The point is that, without that "fringe," the church would not be a church but a sect. One of the fundamental differences between churches and sects is that a sect—unlike a church—is limited to a "hard core" of absolutely identifiable members and in some cases considers that type of member to be the ideal. Churches tend to be older, wiser, more experienced, and more tolerant: they know that they need not just a "hard core," a skeleton, but also a rather more resilient body (and it's all for the best if that body is not undernourished by excessive dieting). Churches tend to integrate people who realize that the notion of core and fringe within an organism like the church is fairly relative—and an analogy with Christ's words that "the last will be first" would seem to be relevant here also.

Once when I was visiting St. Peter's Basilica in Rome, it struck me what a splendid image of the church that cathedral is. It was designed by the architect so that the square—enclosed by a colonnade resembling open arms—is an integral part of the place of worship, in addition to the inner space of the basilica. As soon as people pass through the colonnade and throng through the square—including those who do not enter the door and kneel down inside—they are inside the cathedral, even though most of them are unaware of it. That is precisely what the Catholic Church should look like. If, instead of a colonnade, it built an impenetrable wall, or if it were to actually abandon the space of the square—in which, naturally, it is impossible to demand the disciplined behavior or proper attire required inside the basilica—it would abandon its catholicity. When I observe Catholics who would like to discipline the church's plurality in accordance with their own very quirky concept of Catholicism, I feel sad that these "zealots for the house of the Lord" fail to realize that they are actually dangerous assassins threatening one of the most vital functions of the church, its catholicity—its universality, which should be the ideal of all Christian churches that pray the Apostles' Creed.

ᕙ

Oh God, how I pray for the church to fulfill St. Paul's vision of a body in which all the parts complement each other in their diversity and respect each other's specific purpose, where the eye doesn't say to the hand, or the head doesn't tell the foot, "I do not need you."[3] How I wish that we could realize at last, with all its implications, that "the body of Christ" needs eyes that look progressively ahead, feet that stand firmly on the soil of tradition, hands that intervene actively in the world's affairs, and attentive, hearing ears that silently and contemplatively listen to the beating of God's heart!

ᕙ

Out of all the metaphors that abound in the Old and New Testaments, the Second Vatican Council chose for its theology the image of a community of pilgrims, *communio viatorum,* God's people, journeying through history in the strength of the faith. It also proclaimed that it neither knew nor recognized any definitive boundaries of God's people, that by their very humanity all people, in a certain sense, belong to the mysterious body of the church and the mysterious body of the Crucified. What does that imply for the community of the journey, for the spirituality and ethics of sharing and bearing together "the day and the heat" of the common pilgrimage?

I once read with profound agreement the words written by the writer Gertrud von Le Fort, shortly after her conversion from Protestantism to Catholicism (which was long before the "epoch of ecumenism"), that she did not regard her entry into the Catholic

Church as a rejection of the Protestant church, but rather the linking of two confessions that had been torn apart—that she still saw the Reformation as an act engendered in its day by the Holy Spirit and that she did not consider the Catholic Church as the enemy of the Protestant church, but as its home.[4]

Yes, that's how I myself always considered it, in a country for which the healing reconciliation of the two Christian traditions is painfully important. Were the Catholic Church to utterly reject the contribution of the Reformation it would not be entirely catholic; it would be impoverished. And wherever, on the contrary, Protestantism fails to regard itself as part of the "catholic context," as a complementary element of existing Catholicism, and instead sees itself as its enemy, it loses its roots and depth. I have never perceived ecumenism as a path to a unity or uniformity that would require the denial, suppression, and squandering of so many charismatic differences between the two traditions, but instead as a brotherly encounter in joy and respect, acknowledging the inspirational and enriching variety of their gifts.

But let us move on. Is it possible to regard in like manner the relationship between believing Christians and those who profess a secular belief in humankind and "earthly values"? We have long been traveling through history side by side—perhaps the time has come to reflect on how we might travel the next part of the journey together!

This task has specific significance in the post-Communist countries, where protagonists of both those currents once stood side by side in their opposition to the totalitarian regimes, but in some places their unity and alliance came to an end with the demise of the external enemy. Often it proved impossible to recast the "negative unity" as a "positive unity." Similarly, it is hard to move from "freedom from" to "freedom to," or positive freedom. A society that has freed itself from the grip of totalitarianism is naturally differentiated, and not everyone is able to accept and perceive it as a natural and normal development. Many of those who spent years confronting hostile pressure and defined themselves negatively in relation to oppression are no longer capable of "living without an enemy." They immediately look for enemies to fill the gap—often from the ranks of their former friends and allies.

After the fall of Communism, Christians frequently found a new enemy in the form of "Western liberalism" (and they now happily apply that label to proponents of secular humanism). Secular humanists, for their part, started regarding Christians as enemies of free society who yearned for some kind of "clerical totalitarianism." Those who were once so close—some of them had even been fellow prisoners in Stalinist jails and concentration camps—were now alienated from each other once more.

Democratic society cannot hold its own without the cooperation of Christians and secular humanists; both traditions comprise a very important moral potential, and it is very unfortunate if they waste their efforts on mutual disputes. Besides, even this is not a problem confined to the post-Communist countries. During my most recent visits to the United States, I gained the impression that the relationship between Christians and "secularists" (as well as between left-wing and right-wing Christians), particularly as a result of the "religious Right's" support for Bush's policies and the war in Iraq, had sharpened considerably—although it's hard to say to what degree the expression "culture war" is either appropriate or exaggerated. I consider this a very dangerous signal for the future—not least because the only way the West can convince the more reasonable sections of the Islamic world that it is not the "realm of Satan" is by demonstrating in practice that religion and secular society not only are capable of living together in peace, but that they can also greatly enrich each other.

When I was recently asked to address an all-European conference on the preconditions for cooperation between Christian and secular humanism, I proposed, as I had done that time in the Czech parliament, a meditation on a Gospel story.[5]

The precondition for the mutual existence of the two groups is the understanding and acknowledgment that they need each other, in the same way the brothers in Jesus's best-known parable did. In the parable, the older brother embodies order, the younger one freedom. In his longing for absolute freedom, the younger brother anticipates his father's death (the death of God?), takes his inheritance, and sets off for foreign parts. When he comes to grief, he returns home. The motive for his return is not noble by any means: he is hungry and attracted by the vision of a better life, and is even ready to exchange his status of son for that of a day laborer. Throughout his journey home, he composes a statement of his repentance and repeats it over and over again in his mind: "Father, I have sinned against heaven and against you. I no longer deserve to be called your son; treat me as you would treat one of your hired workers. Father, I have sinned against heaven and against you. I no longer deserve . . ."

He returns home, and now comes the crucial moment not only for him but also for his father and brother. If the father had decided to score a moral victory and hurled reproaches at him, if on his son's return he had said, "Now at last we see who was right!," he would, in a certain sense, have killed his son. He would have lost him forever as a son, and indeed would simply have had one more day laborer. But the father doesn't even let him get the words of repentance out of his mouth and instead hugs him tightly. He has brought his son back to life and saved him by his generous love.

The same moment was also a precious opportunity for the other son's change of heart: if he had accepted his brother in a similar way, there would have really been a happy end; they would both realize that, just as freedom without order will always come to grief, so also order cannot live without freedom. But the older brother is incapable of accepting his brother as a brother and, in his speech to his father (which is full of reproaches and expressions of jealousy), he describes him as "your son": "When your son returns who swallowed up your property with prostitutes . . ." (Incidentally, there is no mention of prostitutes in the story; it is obviously a typical sexual fantasy of the pious projected onto someone else.)

In reply, the father calls the older son "my child." Yes, whereas the younger son has reached adulthood not only through his courage in setting out on an adventure and through his abject failure, but above all due to his change of heart and acceptance, his elder brother, due to his defiance, has remained childish, dependent, and immature. He thinks only of himself and remains centered on his own interests and wishes, not giving any thought to his brother's future. He has written him off in his heart, like Cain; he doesn't feel he is his brother's "keeper"; he doesn't feel responsible for him.

How can this parable be applied to the relationship between Christians and secular humanists? Both currents are "brothers," because they have the same mother—Europe—and the same "grandparents"—the Hebrew faith and the wisdom of antiquity. Today's

"Christian humanism" and secular humanism also have the same father—the Enlightenment, thanks to which Christian humanism is "humanism" and secular humanism inherited the epithet "secular."

If that ambiguous magic word "humanism" is still to retain some positive sense, then let us use it when referring to an attitude to the world that is based on the realization that humans are precisely human and not God, that they have only human powers at their disposal, and a (limited and finite) human perspective. They do not possess "the whole truth" even when they profess a "revealed religion"—they are capable of understanding and accepting God's revelation only as pilgrims in search of the truth, which they recognize "only partially as in a mirror and in parables." Between the Renaissance and the Enlightenment, it was precisely humanism that inferred the appropriate consequences of that attitude that had already been expressed by St. Paul.[6]

From the Christian standpoint, secular humanism is often perceived as the errant younger son, who set off for a distant land in pursuit of a vision of freedom, and now, after his downfall, we anticipate (with almost unconcealed satisfaction) his penitent return. In its sojourn "abroad," in territories distant from the Christian tradition and God, secular humanism undoubtedly fell prey to many evil enticements. Suffice it to recall how easily left-wing intellectuals succumbed to the charms of totalitarian Communism's ideology!

However, in the "Babylonian captivity" of Communist rule, Christians also underwent various adventures, and many of them also failed badly. A lot of them—as is now gradually coming to light—got mixed up with the forces of evil and failed to resist various temptations.

"Back to Europe!" was one of the slogans of the Velvet Revo-

lution in November 1989, almost immediately after the fall of the
Berlin Wall, that symbol of the Iron Curtain whereby Communism
divided the nations of central Europe from the West, to which they
had belonged throughout their culture's thousand-year history.[7] So,
in that sense, both of the sons "go home to Europe," albeit each under the impression—as was indicated, for instance, by the dispute
over the wording to the preamble of the European Constitution—
that he has somewhat greater "right of domicile" than the other.

I think that the greatest test of maturity for us as Christians will
be our ability and willingness to regard the secular humanists of today, not as our enemies, but as our—albeit often irate and not always agreeable—brethren. We should definitely not behave like a
"righteous older brother"! The same applies to the other side also.
There are many scars, injustices, misunderstandings, mutual disappointments, and conflicts in the history of our mutual relations, and
many prejudices and fears still remain. But this is not the time for
recriminations; it is a time for a change of heart and a quest for mutual compatibility.

We are crossing a very narrow bridge from the Communist past
to the united Europe of the future, and the chasm we cross is too deep
and dangerous for the two of us—the proponents of the two versions
of humanism—to wrestle with each other. On the contrary, mutual
support and assistance is what is needed. The first major task we face
as a challenge not only for reflection but also practical action is how
to steer the common European ship between the Scylla of religious
and national fundamentalism and the Charybdis of equally intolerant
secularism, which seeks to displace religion entirely from the public
arena and is itself turning into an intolerant "religion" in the process.

In the past, the Anglo-Saxon world, particularly America, was an example to many Christians that faith and the legacy of the Enlightenment need not conflict. It was precisely the experience of Roman Catholics in America—via such figures as the Jesuit John Courtney Murray or the French philosopher Jacques Maritain, who was very familiar with American society and culture—that gave the Catholic Church at the Second Vatican Council the courage to open up to the modern world and say "yes" to such values as freedom of conscience, democracy, religious tolerance, human rights, and critical rationalism. Will America manage to avert the "culture war" that some people enjoy talking about these days and resist the lures of "fundamentalism" and one-sidedness, both left and right? When I saw the film *The People vs. Larry Flynt,* by my fellow Czech Miloš Forman, everything inside me cried out: *No!* I don't identify with Larry Flynt or with the people who shoot at him! Show us another path at last!

In the same way that freedom and order necessarily belong together, so also do Christian faith and "the legacy of the Enlightenment": secular humanism and critical rationalism. The culture of the West is based precisely on their compatibility. They are brothers who have to complement and correct each other. Faith without critical questions would turn into a tedious and lifeless ideology and infantile bigotry, or fundamentalism and dangerous fanaticism. But rationality without spiritual and ethical impulses, stemming from the world of faith, would likewise be one-sided and dangerous, and could develop into cynical pragmatism or rancorous skepticism.

❧

Let us return, however, to the image of the church that we mentioned at the beginning of these reflections. The Virgin Mother is not the only possible icon of the church; it could also be the passionate woman Mary Magdalene, the apostle to the apostles, who, according to old apocryphal texts, kissed Jesus on the mouth, and also, according to the Gospel, remained with Mary and John beneath the cross after the other disciples fled.

These days Mary Magdalene is courted by journalistic pseudohistorians who write commercial kitsch of the *Da Vinci Code* variety, in which she is transformed through an alchemical melting pot of apocryphal fragments, legends, esoteric writings, and above all unbridled imagination, into the superstar of a quirkily remythologized gospel. But every heresy—and this is what used to be described as a heresy—is "truth gone mad" (Chesterton); every heresy is a theological challenge. There are good reasons to concern ourselves with Mary Magdalene even long after the bestsellers about her offspring with Jesus have been forgotten.

The topicality of Mary Magdalene for the present reflections was revealed to me here at the hermitage on her feast day by the patristic text for that day in the breviary. In it, Pope St. Gregory mentions, among other things, the familiar scene in which Mary Magdalene—after her initial confusion—recognizes the resurrected Christ, and Gregory draws attention to a detail that interestingly links this scene with Jesus's encounter with Zacchaeus (although the author himself does not make that connection): Mary doesn't recognize Jesus until He addresses her as "woman," and the event culminates in the moment when He addresses Mary by name.

In his Homily on the Gospels, Gregory presents her as a paragon and chiefly as an example of patience: patient faith, patient love, patient searching. Mary was the first to see Christ because she patiently remained at the tomb when the others had left.

"Perseverance is essential for any beneficial work, as the voice of truth tells us: Whoever perseveres to the end will be saved," Gregory writes, and continues: "At first she sought but did not find, but when she persevered it happened that she found what she was looking for. When our desires are not satisfied, they grow stronger, and becoming stronger they take hold of their object. Holy desires likewise grow with anticipation, and if they do not grow they are not really desires. Anyone who succeeds in attaining the truth has burned with such a great love. As David says: My soul has thirsted for the living God; when shall I come and appear before the face of God? And so also in the Song of Songs the Church says: I was wounded by love; and again: My soul is melted with love."

After the Battle of White Mountain,[8] the Catholics erected on the former battleground the Church of Our Lady of Victories—an image of the church triumphant, *ecclesia triumfans.* Maybe the other Mary, Mary Magdalene, as she is presented by St. Gregory, could be an image of the seeking church, a church triumphing through its patient seeking and passionate longing. Maybe that image can say more to us nowadays than the first one; if there is any way faith can "triumph" over lack of faith, then it is solely insofar as it displays patience and genuine longing.

CHAPTER 6

ے

A Letter

The night before I left for the hermitage, I tried to read and deal with at least part of the enormous pile of letters that had gradually accumulated on my desk in Prague. I had shelved them there during the previous three weeks, when I was examining students from morning till evening, and when each evening, sometimes until long after midnight, I read their essays and dissertations. But my good intentions foundered when I opened one of the first letters that came to hand.

At first glance the envelope drew my attention because of its bulkiness—surely no one can think I have time to read letters as long as that? The writer introduces himself as a civil engineer and feels he ought to add right away that he is a convinced atheist, indeed an antitheist. His wife is a fervent believer, however, and he regularly reads religious books—even follows the *Catholic Weekly*; he tells me that he has definitely read more theological and spiritual literature from his wife's extensive library than she has herself. He has already read my books, and although he doesn't agree with me in the least, he read them with great interest because they are different from the rest—he values the fact that I try to consider things impartially from different angles, and he says it's obvious that I write what I truly think and feel. That was why he decided to write to me, and he is enclosing an older text of his, should I have the time to read it, because I might find there some alternate answers to the questions I raise, or at the very least could confront my opinions with the way he sees things. He says he doesn't expect a reply.

I realized that if I shelved that manuscript now it would end up sooner or later in the wastebasket. I receive many similar tracts from various private religious wiseacres, who insist that I "assess" and comment on them and always confront me with a very embarrassing dilemma. It is usually obvious from the texts that the author is a sincere spiritual seeker worthy of encouragement, and who, moreover, has often undergone some kind of dramatic conversion or a moment of illumination for which I have absolute respect. But these people apparently don't realize how extremely hard it is to clothe such experiences in words and convey them intelligibly to others. In general, the authors of these texts have had no education in philosophy or theology, so they often use terminology that they are not competent to deal with. The result is dismally reminiscent of the neo-Gnostic pamphlets that cram the bookshop shelves labeled "Esoterica." In answering them, I agonize between the Scylla of insincere politeness and the Charybdis of impolite sincerity. How can I write to someone that their nobility of spirit, their love of truth, and the authenticity of their spiritual experience are beyond all doubt, but the text that they have languished over and promised so much from was not worth the effort?

Even this letter, which eventually attracted me precisely because the writer did not request an answer, did not promise any great spiritual adventure at the outset. At the very beginning of the letter the author proudly proclaimed his atheism and promised that he would make confetti of the Christians' faith, disprove the existence of God, and demonstrate the utter senselessness of the Bible. As a young convert, I always bet militant atheists that I could provide more proofs against the faith and the church than they could, so that fatuous boyish competitiveness was slightly aroused in me. To tell the truth, the text before me made for rather boring reading. Almost any village priest or first-year seminarian could answer all the old threadbare arguments of the Enlightenment philosophers, positivists, and Marxists that I found there. The author could have spared himself the trouble of rolling out example after example of the inconsistencies and contradictions in the Bible, if, instead of outdated catechisms, he had read at least one little book about contemporary biblical hermeneutics, or at least Origen's splendid dictum: "God permitted inconsistencies in the Bible to show us we must not settle for a literal interpretation of scripture, but should always seek its deeper meaning." The inventory of the Inquisition's horrible deeds and of the murky pages of church history were a hotchpotch not only of the "black legends" of Communist propaganda pamphlets, but also of the sad facts of the church's tragic failures, which were acknowledged in penitence on the brink of the new millennium by Pope John Paul II. What more can we do with it at this time? Are the Americans to be morally disqualified for all time because of the way their ancestors treated the Indians, or do present-day Europeans bear guilt for the behavior of the colonizers at the beginning of modern times? If Alexander VI was a scoundrel, is that really an argument against the church as such, or even against faith?

Questions that fall within the realm of theodicy—the theological discipline that deals with the problem of how to reconcile the existence of evil and suffering in the world with belief in a good and omnipotent God—are indeed very hard, and so I had to agree fully with the author that many of the classical theological theories do not provide satisfactory answers. But does atheism? Will these things be clearer to us or will we be better equipped to confront the problem of evil and suffering if we reach the conclusion that there is no God? The world is ambiguous and full of paradoxes. We have to decide responsibly which of the alternate explanations we choose. You chose the one, I chose the other—what more is there to discuss, my dear sir? I enjoy provocative critics of religion, such as Nietzsche, sparkling with original ideas and provoking new thinking about faith. I like those who show us just how complex are the problems between faith and nonfaith, and whose comments don't allow faith to become torpid or complacent. I like it when someone puts me in a position where I have run out of arguments and I am obliged once more to lean out over the thrilling chasm of mystery. But so far this text contained nothing of the kind. Far from it—it was just the usual shallow, hackneyed, naive, self-assured atheism that was the spitting image of many silly pamphlets by religious apologists.

Atheism can be interesting and stimulating in its critical function. It becomes remarkably boring and sterile when it transforms itself into a dogmatic metaphysics, as happened to positivist materialism and Marxism. It can be useful as an opponent, paradoxically living from faith and reliant on it as an inverted theology, but by and large it doesn't build anything positive on its own account. (Then again, one might say that theology—not faith as such, but its intellectual elaboration—"lives on heresy" in a sense and to a certain degree, and needs it as an indispensable opponent.)

Why did the man send it to me, I thought? Does he really want to convert me and turn me overnight into that type of atheist? Does he take me for an idiot who's unable to answer arguments of that kind and think my faith is such a frail dwelling that it will collapse like a house of cards after ten pages of such outpourings? Or does he feel the need to bolster his own opinions this way, fearing unconsciously that his skepticism might not be so consistent, and that it might end up becoming—as it once did with me—skepticism about his own skepticism, relativizing his own relativism?

I was about to throw the tract into the wastebasket when my eye was drawn to its continuation, obviously written at a different date and in quite a different tone. In it, God, whose existence has just been disproved conclusively and for good and all by the author (in his own eyes, at least), is suddenly subjected to the most extraordinary invective, concluding with the words: "You're a tyrant with bloody claws. I curse you!"

Even for me, who once served as adviser to the Pontifical Council for Dialogue with Non-Believers, cursing God was a bit "over the top," so I started to read the text again, trying to discover in the pages that I had skipped the reason why he discreetly resurrected the God he'd already successfully done away with, in order to take Him to task in this drastic fashion. I found the crucial paragraph—and it completely altered my attitude to the text and to its author. In it, the writer discloses that a little granddaughter of his died of cancer. The entire preceding text had obviously been a rationalization, camouflaging what the author declares in those two dreadful closing sentences. Previously he had spoken in the borrowed language of pamphlets; now he spoke in his own voice of a grievously wounded heart. I immediately felt ashamed of all the irony with which I had previously read the text. Human pain, even when it is clothed in the armor of militant atheism, is something that Christians must take seriously and treat with respect, because it is "hallowed ground."

With his litanies of atheist arguments, was the man trying to take revenge on God for the loss he had suffered? Did he really want to trample God into nonexistence? Or had the vacuum left by the God whose nonexistence he had so intricately proved been immediately filled by the "tyrant with bloody claws," the very God he needed on whom to vent his rage, because yelling into a total void is even more wretched?

Am I to write to him that the "tyrant with bloody claws" really does not exist, that the arguments with which he'd just filled so many sheets of paper were all true as regards that monster? A god like that truly does not exist—we are in total agreement on that score! But what is his prospect now? Will it help him to think that the death of his granddaughter was just an "accident," an absurdity without any meaning at all? Will it help him to be advised not to seek any deeper meaning in her death, to simply content himself with the medical explanation of the malignant process that causes the death of such and such a number of people according to statistics, and simply suppress the unanswerable questions: "Why me of all people?" "Why her of all people?" Did it come as a relief for him to find in God a culprit into whose face he could yell all his pain because he could find no other culprit? And even if he found one— a doctor who had diagnosed the condition too late, or the mother who failed to seek medical advice in time—could he use the same tone with impunity when speaking to them?

Is it part of God's service to humanity that he "turns the other cheek," that he puts up with a cry that is even harsher than Job's indictment—or had God really hidden his face from this atheist, so that he wrestled with only a projection of his own horror and pain?

Or had that man never in fact encountered the Gospel, so that his religious world was actually the world of ancient tragedy, where all events in the world of humans are directly controlled by gods, and implacable Fate rules over gods and man alike? A Promethean revolt against the gods may have made some sense there. But the God of the Bible is not a cold-blooded director of our destinies, hidden somewhere behind the scenes of the historical stage. He personally entered the history of our misfortune and drained the cup of our pain to its dregs; He knows all too well the weight of our crosses! Why revile a God who does not intervene in our lives like a *deus ex machina* in the dramas of antiquity, a God to whom we have access solely through the one who took upon himself the fate of a servant, "who came in human likeness,"[1] who "was accustomed to suffering"?[2] After all, Christianity does not offer us a God who is to provide us with a life without adversity or who will immediately provide satisfactory answers to all the painful questions that adversity raises in our hearts, nor does it promise days that will not be followed by night. All He assures us is that, in those profoundest nights, He is with us, so that this assurance itself should give us the strength not only to bear their darkness and burden, but also to help others to bear it, particularly those who have not heard or accepted His assurance.

Did that man write his dismal atheist tract before that event and is now perhaps assailed by the subconscious dread that this was God's punishment? Although such things seem scarcely credible, I have been amazed in the past to discover that many atheists implicitly or unconsciously harbor very peculiar and often quite pathologically

functioning quasi-theological constructs and primitive religious notions. There is a Czech play in which the protagonist declares that
he is such a convinced atheist that he is often afraid that God will
punish him for it. The play is a comedy and the members of the audience naturally laugh their heads off at this humorous comment.
They would be amazed how many "atheists," particularly those who
frantically suppressed their childish faith as the result of some
trauma, really entertain such subconscious anxieties.

And there are many people who long maintained a childish notion of a magic god, a god of banal consolations and superficial optimism, a "guardian angel" at our service, an inveterate comforter
who tells us everything will turn out all right, a household god intended to fulfill just one single role: "working" as an infallible
granter of our most fatuous wishes. Cozy little gods like that logically collapse when faced with the first serious crises of our lives.
After taking leave of a god of that variety, quite a lot of people—
often with a certain pride in discovering the truth about the "real
world" at last—declare themselves to be "atheists." They have
clearly not come across a Christian, Jew, or Muslim who would
congratulate them on their discovery that "God doesn't work," that
this projection of our infantile yearning for unlimited power (under
the protection of a great ally behind the scenes of the world stage)
is an idol, and that by toppling it they now find themselves in the
anteroom of a possible encounter with the living God, the God of
Abraham's pilgrim faith.

Maybe that tragic event did, after all, cause my correspondent
to shift from naive atheism to a tussle with God. Did he realize that
by lambasting God he had in fact entered the territory of faith? The
whole Bible is full of testimonies to the fact that God has a soft spot

for those who tussle with him, as Polish theologian Father Józef Tischner used to say.

Manifestly, it is truly dreadful, hopeless, and maybe even impossible to suffer without God. To suffer without a counterpart, in the abyss of anonymous absurdity, blind chance, or inexorable fate that is faceless and heartless, that cannot even hear my crying, or my protest and anger. That is why, in the depths of suffering, some "unbelievers" first hear the voice of God, who spoke to Job out of the whirlwind and the tempest and to Elijah in the gentle breeze. But there are others—mostly those with less patience—who, at moments like these, "create their own god" just in order to have something to confront, most frequently on the bench of the accused. If one can find a culprit for one's misfortune and can put him on trial, it alleviates somewhat the absurdity and senselessness of the misfortune. At this point, one is in a more or less familiar situation that one can deal with, and thus avoid the murky depths of the impenetrable and unintelligible. Better a "tyrant with bloody claws" than an unfathomable and unnameable void!

But one cannot live for very long with a "tyrant with bloody claws" or other "homemade" gods. They are bogeymen, and nothing but bogeymen. It is necessary to cast them out or eradicate them from within you. In some people, atheism, "the killing of God," and aversion to religion are the result of that very act—they get rid of a god of that kind, whether it was one they previously created themselves out of the pathological sediment of pain and anxiety or one they "inherited," because it is, alas, possible to hand on perverse gods of this kind to others (particularly children) through upbringing or a certain type of preaching.

For that matter, this was possibly true in Nietzsche's case. His notion of God would seem to have been burdened since childhood by that fateful, traumatic dream in which—shortly after his father's death—he saw his father arise from his tomb to the sound of an organ, return home, and fetch from there a little child, which he carried back with him to the grave. Nietzsche confides that the following morning, after he awoke from that dreadful, anguished dream, his little younger brother suddenly died. Is it possible that a mixture of anxiety and guilt that his dead father had carried his brother away to the grave instead of him got stuck in the child's subconscious? Doesn't such a "father god," threatening the living from beyond the grave, deserve to be killed at last—in order "to be dead and stay dead," as the madman in Nietzsche's *Gay Science* proclaims?[3]

To abandon a religion of that kind and have the courage to eradicate such a god from within oneself is undoubtedly a positive step. But where to from there? The question remains: "Master, to whom shall we go?" (John 6:68)

I realized that until his pain had subsided I must not simply say to the man who had written to me, "God loves you." There are some truths that, if stated at the wrong moment, not just become embarrassingly empty clichés, but can actually give offense and wound. Initially, Job's friends sat in silence with the sufferer day and night—and if they had kept it up and not succumbed to the foolish temptation to make him the object of their "pastoral care," they would probably have spared themselves the Lord's harsh rebuke toward the end of the book, where God interrupts their pious speculations and vindicates solely Job, who wrangled with him and called him to judgment.

I still haven't replied to this letter, and I'm not sure whether it is due to cowardice, laziness, weakness, and the irresoluteness of my own faith and theology, or whether I judged correctly that any words in this phase could only pour more oil on the flames and salt in the wound. If I didn't live so far away, I expect I would have gone to see him and gripped his hand in mine. "Where was God when your granddaughter was dying? I don't know," I'd tell him truthfully. "But at this moment, I'd like you to feel Him in the hand gripping yours."

ॐ

"Who is my neighbor?" they asked Jesus—trying to make Him name clear boundaries. Is it only the upright Jew, fulfilling his religious duties—or maybe also the sinner and the customs officer like Zacchaeus? Is it only a Jew, or maybe also someone from among our uncircumcised neighbors?

And Jesus, as is His wont, told a story—the parable of the Good Samaritan. And the moral of the story, the answer to the question asked, which Jesus eventually provoked the questioner himself to provide by His counterquestion, is: Turn yourself into a neighbor. There is no need to speculate about who your neighbor is; you don't need a guru to give you an answer. The answer is for you to determine, by your deeds, by your attitudes, and with them you can cross any frontiers. By overcoming your selfishness, by being close to people—particularly in their need—you can turn people into your neighbors, and you can go on widening the area of your neighborhood without boundaries.

People wanted to hear what signs on earth, on the sun, and in the stars would accompany the arrival of God's Kingdom, and sometimes Jesus seemed to indulge their impatience. But on one occasion He told them: God's rule is already among you. It was among them in the person of Jesus, above all in His love transcending all boundaries.

Wherever we follow in His footsteps by bringing others closer to us, including those "at a distance," the rule of God on earth is widened. The Holy Thursday liturgy, when the celebrant fulfills Jesus's command that "you also ought to wash one another's feet," sings about this in the words of the ancient sequence: "Where there is love there is God."

ॐ

But where is God when there is no love, when there is just cruelty, pain, sin, and suffering? He is there in the patient faith and hope of those who, in such situations, have not allowed themselves to be overcome by evil. Cruelty, pain, and indifference not only have their perpetrators, they always have their victims, although we do not always see or want to see them. Victims of violence can always be drawn into the circle of malice by a longing for revenge, but they can also reject that sinister longing. Victims of pain are tempted by malice or resignation, but can also surmount that temptation in the end and come to terms with such states of mind.

Maybe, in some cases, it is expecting too much to ask love and joy of victims in the midst of pain and hatred. But perhaps they can show patience. As we said at the very outset, patience comprises two fundamental aspects of faith: trust and faithfulness. In certain situations, faith and patience are only different names for the same attitude.

And if love can imply or "stand in for" faith—as we saw in the case of the dying Thérèse de Lisieux—then maybe patient faith can also wait for the night of hatred or pain to pass, and thereby at least pave the way for love. Yes, it can pave the way, but it is as hard to hasten or force the onset of love and joy as to summon the dawn at night.

It is only here, in the silence, that it occurs to me that maybe the only reason that man sent me his dreadful letter in which God is cursed, and for which he sought no reply, was because somewhere, in the depths of his soul, he sensed or hoped that I would pray for him. Maybe he too is Zacchaeus, gazing from a distance, and I was supposed to bring closer to him the One who, more than anyone else, understood human pain.

And so I really have been praying for him here in the hermitage. What do I pray for? For his "conversion" in the sense that he should substitute my views on religion for his own? I think that would be a bit presumptuous. I pray that he should be given the gift of patience, so that the hopelessness of pain, anger, and curses will not be the last word in his communication with God, to whom, after all, he has devoted much time and effort—much more than many of the pious. It struck me today—and it made me smile, because it really is something I could not write to him at this time— that if he were to direct all that energy in a rather different direction, if he really were granted the gift of "patience with God" and used it, he has the makings of a saint. In all events, who knows where his journey will take him?

⟡

Yes, the lengthy confession of that old atheist did really only start to interest me when I discovered that his final, blasphemous sentence came from somewhere much deeper than those hackneyed arguments of Enlightenment reason: they sprang from a wounded heart. It was the "passionate atheism" in which the Christian who is a child of Kierkegaard—that prophet of passionate faith as a bold leap from certainty into the very heart of paradox—recognizes a brother!

There exist passionate atheism and the atheism of apathy, just as there exist passion and apathy in the world of religion. There is little point in wasting much time on the atheism of indifference, which is simply not interested in the question of God, because it doesn't fit into its world of "scientific certainties" or material security, unless, perhaps, we have "reasonable suspicion" that those certainties simply mask an inner restlessness; beware, it might only be a projection of our own desires.

The atheism of apathy is just as tedious as the apathetic idle faith that finds a cozy home, with its habits and certainties, in the "inheritance of the fathers," in the treasure that it carefully buries and has no intention—like the good-for-nothing, idle servant in Jesus's parable of the talents—of risking or investing in the game for fear of losing something. This kind of faith also does nothing to increase the treasure and, as Jesus warns, at the final accounting it will lose everything; even what it has will be taken away.

Passionate atheism assumes at least two different forms: the passion of protests and the passion of seeking. In this book, little Zacchaeus from Luke's Gospel has been made a symbol of seekers on account of his inquisitive watching from the foliage. If people explicitly seek God and declare themselves to be atheists because they haven't found him in anything offered by the religious institutions and doctrines they have encountered, then what I aim at here is to call into doubt not their seeking, but rather their previous self-understanding and their self-designation as atheists. I would like to tell them that they are "atheists" only in respect of a certain type of religion and its adherents (and perhaps only in their eyes), that they are opponents of idle religion—but that they are (even in opposition to this form of religion) allies, neighbors, and associates of Augustine, Pascal, Kierkegaard, and thousands of others for whom faith is precisely a constant and passionate journey toward God that cannot and must not end on this earth. On the other hand, let's not drag these seekers onto our side too hastily. Let us respect the rhythm of their journey. Let us respect their self-understanding and give them the time and freedom to decide when—and if ever—they want to take the step of "name change." Let us bear in mind that all are invited, none must be forced!

The passionate seekers also include those who never regard their seeking as a search for God, as religious seeking. They might speak in terms of seeking the truth, meaning, justice, love. Most likely they would say nothing rather than risk profaning their seeking and its "object" in front of others and themselves by employing such "grandiose" and fervent expressions, which have often been drained of meaning to the point of kitsch or banality. Yes, in these people too our Augustinian, Pascalian, or Kierkegaardian faith—this style of understanding and living Christianity—sees its substantive allies. It regards them as brothers and sisters who (maybe from another direction, along a different path, according to a different map and on a different rope) are clambering up to the same steep peak, which for all of us is covered at this moment in clouds, so that we have rather different notions and expectations regarding its precise shape. It is possible and even probable that we and they will eventually be surprised—and not only by whom we'll (perhaps) meet there at the end. But it equally applies to these people that we should offer them our friendship and our closeness. Let us openly demonstrate our conviction that we are brothers, albeit without indulging in rash, arrogant, or intrusive proselytism, without "poaching," without hastily claiming others as our own (something that the great Jewish thinker Emmanuel Levinas warned against). Passionate people recognize each other instinctively, in the same way that it is hard for two people in love to conceal the fact, however much they try. Yet let us not impair the right and freedom of others to call their passion by whatever name they choose.

Within the "atheists' camp," one does not solely encounter "passionate seeking," however. There is also passionate protest and passionate hate. Sometimes I take a look at Internet chats, but it is a harrowing experience—all the dreadful hatred and malevolence that the slightest mention of God and belief, or church and religion, arouses in so many people, hidden in anonymity or behind pseudonyms, and only rarely daring to append their real name. How many crimes committed against Christians have already found weaponry on these plains of prejudice and malevolence, so reminiscent of the anti-Semitic malice that smoldered for millennia in the consciousness or unconsciousness of many Christians until a neo-pagan ideology fanned it into the inferno of the Holocaust?

But even here I seek to understand. Did not St. Ignatius of Loyola teach us to strive to the very bounds of possibility to ascribe the best intentions to our neighbor's every act? Malice and hatred are undoubtedly dangerous vices; but sometimes the rhetoric and the feelings of hatred conceal something else: the passion of protest.

At various places in this book, the point is made that the fanaticism of antireligious hatred can be a frantic attempt to drown out the atheists' unconscious doubts—concealed even from themselves—about their lack of faith, in the same way that the fanaticism of believers tends to be a substitute battle with their own unacknowledged religious doubts. The biographers of Sigmund Freud relate his hostility toward church religion—which occasionally veers away emotionally from would-be impartial, strictly rational academic analysis—to his "temptation to sign up with the church" (get baptized), which he mentions in his correspondence (whether it stemmed from a hope of greasing the wheels of his academic career and social acceptance in the Vienna of those days or from a memory of his "second mother," his Catholic nurse, and his own childish fascination with the world of Catholicism, as emerged at the time of his self-analysis).[4]

Yes, the rhetoric of hatred often tends to be pain, injury, passionate "indictments of God"—such as I found in that letter. It tends to be the cry of pain and protest. People painfully sense the "injustice" and "undeservedness" of the evil that has overtaken them, and they protest it. But here we come to the hidden paradox of that passionate atheism of protest: the very premise of a predetermined just, meaningful, and good order in the world, one in which only the good are rewarded and only the wicked are punished, is, as Nietzsche rightly perceived, a religious premise—and hence even protest against it operates within the same religious ambit.[5] It would be absurd, after all, if the person protesting against the violation of this order had already denied that order's very existence. If we didn't recognize this order and did not believe in its existence, what would then be the sense of protesting against evil and injustice—in relation to what could some event be "unjust" or "evil"?

If someone wanted to be a consistent atheist, he either would have to be a stoic, putting up with everything; or—as Dostoyevsky perceptively analyzed it—would probably seek, like Ivan Karamazov, by some means (most consistently by suicide) to "return his ticket into this world"; or alternatively could attempt—like Dostoyevsky's "Demons" (and those who have really implemented that vision in history)—to take the world totally under his own control. An atheistic protest against God and belief itself stands on the soil of belief in a divine order of goodness and justice, and it actually confirms and acknowledges that belief by that pain and protest. If I want to curse God, I have to believe in His existence at the very least— so that I can then reproach Him for not being a god in accordance with my own wishes and criteria, for failing to live up to my notions of how He should behave. If I then decide to "reject God," all I have rejected is my own (often unwitting) religious illusion. I stand at a crossroads where I can either consider life one gigantic absurdity (which can result in resignation and cynicism), or, in defiance of the darkness, remain open with patience and trust to a possible ray of light—having rejected "the god who fulfills my wishes" in order to find the courage to trust God the Mystery, and seek rather to understand His wishes and fulfill them. Belief in the living God is by its nature a dialogue in which there is also scope for cries of protest. Often it is only via many crises and much searching that one learns to live in the presence of mystery, to bear even one's own doubts, and finally to allow God the freedom to be a real God, often radically different from the "god of our dreams."

A consistent atheist belief would have to immediately stop the mouth of any protest against the injustice of life—after all, it would be a "protest without an addressee."

But anyone who tried to stifle within himself any protest against evil, pain, and painful issues could hardly remain truly human. The stoicism of consistent atheism would demonstrate hardness of heart and a closed mind, rather than the wisdom of one in the know. Sooner or later, it would probably turn into conformism with this world, the atheism of indifference—and indifference about the issue of God could easily turn into indifference toward painful issues and the pain of the human heart. Indifferent but truly consistent atheism of that variety would truly be the antithesis of a seeking faith—but it would probably come to resemble more and more that "lazy religion," de facto a dead faith, which also rejects all existential questions lest they disrupt the tranquillity of its own certainties.

A seeking faith, on the other hand, can have a fellow feeling with the atheism of pain, passion, and protest. We too sometimes find ourselves face to face with the mystery of evil in the pain of unanswered questions; our faith too resists resting in the peace of final answers, even if these answers were the tawdry comfort of "religious opium" or stoic acceptance of the world's senselessness. We too know that we are only pilgrims, and we view truly satisfactory answers only from afar, as in a mirror (i.e., in an inverted image), in riddles and parables. Our faith too sometimes takes the form of a dispute with God, as when Jacob wrestled with Him in the dark by the stream called Jabbok. Jacob, of course, was victorious. At the height of the contest, at the moment of catharsis in that nocturnal drama, he held his opponent in his grip and begged (nay, compelled) Him to give him His blessing—but he was wounded.

There is only one way for us to conquer this passionate atheism of protest, and that is by embracing it. Let us embrace it with the passion of our faith and bless it: let us make its existential experience part of our own. We cannot obtain the blessing of maturity unless our faith takes seriously the human experience of the tragedy and pain, and unless it bears that experience without belittling it with facile religious comforts. Mature belief is patient dwelling in the night of mystery.

In the contest with atheism—a contest that will not end as a result of disdainful rejection, cunning polemics, slick arguments, or intellectual arrogance, but will culminate in an embrace, recognizing the passion of this unbelief as sister to the passion of our belief— we may be wounded like Jacob and become "limping pilgrims." Mature faith is always faith wounded by the world's suffering. We recognize it by its scars—in the same way that the resurrected Christ identified Himself to His apostles with His scars. Yes, only in this way and at this cost can we acquire a new name, a name denoting the chosen people: the one who contended and prevailed.

CHAPTER 7

Unknown Yet Too Close

The Bible story about Zacchaeus has a happy end: Zacchaeus had a change of heart, he decided to give half of his property to the poor and to make generous reparations to anyone he had cheated, and salvation came to his house. But Zacchaeus's life did not end there. What happened next? The Gospel doesn't tell us. So we are free to think up our own apocrypha about it.

Let us assume that Zacchaeus really did everything he promised. The "little man" grew in his own eyes and in the eyes of his neighbors. His new life brought him a lot of joy and satisfaction: such encounters with Jesus are certainly not forgotten overnight. Jesus did not invite him to become one of His followers as He had his colleague, Matthew, the tax collector. Zacchaeus did not become a traveling apostle, and he didn't write a gospel. He remained true to his profession and tried to do his job well. Can the converted sinner be called Jesus's disciple, or did he instead remain a sympathizer, who just frequently recalled with gratitude his benefactor and stood up for Him whenever Jesus cropped up in conversations with his neighbors?

It is not easy to base one's daily life solely on something that once happened. And so in time even Zacchaeus's enthusiasm became covered in the dust of everyday cares. It's not that he abandoned Jesus, but he didn't think about Him quite as often as before. After all, didn't the Master Himself say that each day has enough trouble of its own? One day, the news of Jesus's trial and execution reached Jericho. Zacchaeus was filled with fear and sorrow. He was heart-stricken and confused, and when he got to hear the stories going around about Jesus's empty tomb and how He had apparently shown Himself to his disciples, his confusion was only compounded. One evening he climbed his fig tree once again to settle his thoughts and emotions amid its foliage.

And during the summer evenings he returned there again and again, until his family and friends started to find it eccentric. "He's waiting for Jesus," they would say, and not without irony. Was he really waiting? We don't know what was taking place in his head and heart. One thing is certain, Jesus never again appeared on the road between Jericho and Jerusalem. Is it possible for Zacchaeus to be called a second time?

౨

Our entire civilization is possibly in a somewhat similar situation. Jesus once passed this way and addressed us by name. But that is a long time ago already. While many traces of His ministry are still evident, others have long been covered by the dust of forgetting. We have heard Nietzsche's message that "God is dead." Many were confused by it, while others were not even jogged out of their complacency. But there are still Zacchaeuses around, seated eccentrically in their solitary hidden observation posts. Will they ever be "called by

name" again? Is it possible to breathe new life into a tired faith—
into the faith of individuals and into the spiritual climate of our
communities and societies?

༈

During my many years' practice as a spiritual director, I have come
to know a good number of people whose enthusiasm for the faith
was once incandescent. It was the faith of their childhood, imbued
with the scents of a safe home, or a faith that once caught fire and
burst into flame like a tree struck by lightning. But "time"—and how
many things are concealed behind that multivalent term—again
smothered almost everything in ash. Their faith now only smolders.

Sometimes they try to do a convulsive somersault backward to
the faith of their own childhood and its simple truths, or to their
own notions about the infancy of the church: let's flee from the
confusion of today's complexities to the unshakable certainties of the
past! But you can't enter the water that has already flowed away in
the river of time. Playing at the past—one's own past or the past of
the church—won't bring back that past or resurrect its reputedly
unshakable certainties; it will simply stir up a slough of illusions and
produce tragicomic caricatures. And even if it were possible to summon up that past again, it would only give rise to shocking disappointment: even those earlier centuries were not free of tension.
Many imperfections, conflicts, and problems of the past were simply censored out by our romantic fantasies that created a fictitious
"golden age of the faith." Most likely there never was any "golden
age of the faith"—every day, every age, and every culture has its
own cares, problems, and dark sides.

Weariness with their faith leads some to seek activities that are offered vociferously by various "new religious movements," particularly those that try to drown out rational questions with impassioned emotions and the persuasive power of mass rallies. But doesn't it occur to them that those spectacular miracles and healings at stadiums are tellingly reminiscent of what Satan tempted Jesus with in the desert and which Jesus resolutely rejected? Are they not likely to suffer disappointment and a painful sobering up, like those who escape from their problems through drugs?

Others try to renew the purity and fervor of their faith by projecting all their own problems and doubts onto others—now they can reject, condemn, and extirpate them! Many of the self-appointed inquisitors of past and present, who have fought passionately against "heretics," were recruited from among those who were unable to admit and bear their own doubts and tried to rid themselves of them by "the mechanism of projection." Luckily for them, the struggle with the "enemies of faith" is unending, because if they ever managed to eradicate every single one and were left all on their own, they would at last be prey to their own demons, who would come back home "and the last condition of that person is worse than the first."[1]

Many people these days, as we mentioned earlier, try to foist responsibility for the weakness of their own faith onto the church (i.e., the hierarchy, the institution) and become its bitterest critics or frantic reformers of its institutional structures, or, alternatively, withdraw from it in frustration. I have already devoted an entire chapter to the church—I really do not underrate it. But I get the impression that its radical critics and its equally agitated apologists resemble each other insofar as they somewhat overrate its importance, particularly of its visible, institutional aspect. If someone "wearies of the church"—which I fully understand sometimes—must this weariness develop into weariness with their faith?

み

Several years ago extensive research was carried out into the value orientation of contemporary Europeans. One of its theological commentators wrote: "God is no longer a self-evident God and has become an alien, unknown God."[2] I reacted to it in a lecture, in which I asked myself and my listeners the question whether this does not represent a great and so far unused opportunity for Christianity.[3]

I recalled the well-known scene from the Acts of the Apostles of Paul's sermon at the Areopagus in Athens.[4] Paul first praises the Athenians for their devoutness in erecting altars to so many gods, so that they even remember "an unknown god," whose altar had particularly intrigued him when he was strolling through the sacred garden. Bible commentators continue to argue over whether these words of praise for "pagan idolatry"—quite unusual from the lips of a devout Jew—were a rhetorical *captatio benevolentiae* (an attempt to win the listeners' favor) or instead an expression of caustic irony.

Paul proceeds to interpret this "unknown god": "What therefore you unknowingly worship, I proclaim to you" (Acts 17:23). This god is not one of the gods that was perhaps forgotten and so is to be honored just to be on the safe side, to prevent him showing anger and taking vengeance; it is the Creator and Lord of heaven and earth. Immediately afterward there comes Paul's critique of idolatry—this God does not dwell in material temples and requires no human rituals; after all, divinity is not some human artifact or material object. Idolatry, Paul says, is an expression of ignorance. God had long tolerated this immature attitude, whereby people related to Him, but now the situation had changed radically and the time had come for repentance.

Paul talks about the Greeks' worship of gods in a similar spirit of censure and irony as was used by the prophets of Israel or by the ancient philosophers when criticizing primitive religious anthropomorphism. Nonetheless, he finds for them a certain time-contingent tolerance; maybe he implicitly accepts the "period of ignorance"—the era of pagan religions—as a kind of pedagogical preparation for the coming of Christ, rather in the way he refers in his letters to the Law of Moses.

Here he speaks about the true God, the one unknown to the Greeks, more in philosophical categories and in terms of poetic piety (*eusebeia*) than in terms of religion as a cult. His speech to the Athenians, with its references to the Greek poets, might even recall a certain sort of pantheism or, at the very least, panentheism: *"He is not far from any of us,"* Paul says. *"For in Him we live and move and have our being. . . . For we too are His offspring"* (Acts 17:27–28). Paul, however, preaches God the Creator—this God created the world and its order ("He fixed the ordered seasons and the boundaries of their regions")—in order to provoke people's religious search "so that all nations might seek the deity and, by feeling their way toward Him, succeed in finding Him." This is a very powerful assertion: that the purpose of creation is a religious quest!

There is something else we should note, though: an "unknown" God is not a distant God. On the contrary, He is incredibly close to us: "in Him we live, and move." *He is unknown not because He is too far away but because He is too close.* After all, we know least of all about what is closest to us, what is most proper to us, what we take for granted. None of us has seen our own face—we only see its image in a mirror. And we can only see God in a mirror; elsewhere Paul states in so many words that during our lives we see God only partly: "indistinctly, as in a mirror," but after death we will see Him "face to face."

Paul wants to show the Athenians the "face" of the unknown God, who is too close, *as mirrored in the story of Jesus of Nazareth,* above all His paradoxical climax: the cross and resurrection. But he does not get that far. When Paul says the words "resurrection from the dead," some of the Athenians start to sneer, while others walk off, having lost interest: they have understood the resurrection as *something they were naturally familiar with,* whether as an absurd fable, or as a frequent image in the mythology of the surrounding nations, where gods frequently died and rose from the dead; the Greek gods, however, enjoy one—and often only one—privilege not accorded humans, and which sets them apart: their immortality.

I will reflect later on how Paul's sermon about the face of God in the mirror of the Easter story might have continued. For the moment, let us linger a bit more at the "altar to an unknown god." Is the fact that the apostle starts his sermon by referring to the "altar to an unknown god" simply a sign of Paul's oratorical quick-wittedness, or does it mean something more?

I am sure that what happened on the Areopagus is paradigmatic in its way. *The "altar to an unknown god" is precisely the most appropriate "topos" for proclaiming the Christian message.* For Paul, as a Jew and a Christian, the only true God is the God that can't be portrayed, one hidden in mystery. A known god is no god at all. It is not surprising that the ancient world—a "world full of gods"—for centuries regarded the Jews and Christians as atheists.

I am convinced that if anyone wants to preach the Good News of the paradoxical God of the Bible, he has to find the "altar to an unknown god." To speak about Christ at the altar to familiar gods would be blasphemy or risk even greater misunderstanding than on that occasion at the Athenian Areopagus.

The world is full of familiar, known gods. Martin Luther said rightly that whatever people assign the greatest value to is their god.[5] Paul himself wrote about "greedy people" as "idolaters" who have "no inheritance in the kingdom of Christ and of God."

The thought occurs to me whether we Christians have not in the course of history constantly fallen prey to the temptation to exchange the paradoxical God of Christ's Easter story for a "familiar god" conforming to the human notions and expectations of specific epochs. Wasn't the identification of the biblical God with the god of the ancient philosophers as described by Plato and Aristotle—so fateful for the history of Christian theology—precisely one of those substitutions?

And if this has happened, and our Christian thinking is burdened with this legacy, then is not much of what we call secularization, criticism and undermining of religion, atheism, etc., no more than taking leave of the *familiar, known gods* and thus a great opportunity to clean and open up a space in which we may hear anew Paul's message? Is not the situation in which, for a large proportion of Europeans, God is an unknown and alien god a summons to a "new Areopagus"?

⳾

In my lecture at that time, in place of an answer I offered another story that was written eighteen centuries after Paul's sermon on the Areopagus. In some respects it is strikingly similar to the scene from Acts and in others quite the opposite. Paul, as we heard, left the Areopagus having persuaded most of his crowd of listeners that he was a madman. To another crowd, in another marketplace, comes another madman to speak about an unknown god. In the chapter entitled "Madman" (*Der tolle Mensch*) of Friedrich Nietzsche's *Gay Science,* a man comes searching for God in the daylight with a lantern, like Diogenes searching for man, but, unlike Paul, *he comes among those who do not believe in God.* Maybe they still talk about him, maybe they even continue to attend his churches (which the madman quickly declares the "mausolea of the dead god") but in reality they are not concerned with him at all and they don't miss him in the least.

This detail in that well-known and celebrated text is often overlooked: the madman, who comes as a herald of God's death, comes to provoke not believers but unbelievers—Nietzsche uses his message to question their matter-of-fact atheism. The people mock the seeker after God, because they have long ceased to seek Him. "Is he hiding? Is he afraid of us? Has he gone on a voyage?" they scoff at the mad seeker from their standpoint of the certainties of "practical atheism." And they cannot understand at all his plaintive message about *why* there is now "no God": "We have killed him, you and I!"

Those for whom God simply does not exist, is not and never was, and those for whom—with equal matter-of-factness—God has "existed" from the beginning of time as an unchanging metaphysical entity, must necessarily find the message about the *death of God* equally insane and incomprehensible as the Athenians did Paul's message of the resurrection.

It was possible to remind the Athenians that divinity was the most intimate part of their *Lebenswelt,* so close and commonplace that they don't even notice it anymore, just as we are unaware of the smell of our home when we are in it all the time. Europeans in the postmodern marketplace would be told that *they no longer live in the sacrosanct*—God's absence (concealed by unthinking conventional atheism or conventional religiosity) has become so axiomatic to them that its cause and effect need to be demonstrated dramatically. "All of us are his murderers. But how did we do this? How could we drink up the sea? Who gave us the sponge to wipe away the entire horizon? What were we doing when we unchained this earth from its sun? . . . Whither are we moving?"

The herald of the death of God in Nietzsche's story does not come in order to bring about his listeners' conversion to atheism, to turn them into atheists at last, perhaps. They are up to their ears in atheism, although they are obviously unaware of it, because God doesn't interest them. The madman, the fool—the only person traditionally permitted to speak unpleasant truths—comes instead to *arouse in them responsibility for the unacknowledged or forgotten reason for their atheism.* The madman (and Nietzsche in his guise) is not seeking to "propagate" atheism and *bring about the death of God* in the minds of his listeners, but has instead come to spread the news that this event has already occurred and to explain its meaning; he wants his listeners to realize how fundamentally this event concerns them. They are the joint victims and joint perpetrators of the death of God.

This deed, apparently committed unwittingly, casually, or at the very least thoroughly displaced into the unconscious, is "too great" for its perpetrators to accept and to grasp its shocking implications *either as a fault* for which they must accept responsibility *or even as a liberating opportunity* that they have to seize; they are quite simply incapable of understanding the message at all. The madman is mad because *he came too early*—thus spake Nietzsche, who undoubtedly identified with this figure whose prophecy was ahead of its time. In his time "ears had not yet grown" for this message.

જ઼

Our ears are full of the tidings about the death of God that have been repeated over and over again since Nietzsche. But what sense have we made of them—and what conclusions have we drawn from the message?

Few sentences admit such a wide range of different and often contradictory interpretations. In *The Gay Science* itself, Nietzsche hints at its ambivalence. In the madman's sermon, the tragic consequences of God's death tend to be stressed: we are hurtling into a dark space far from all suns; we have lost our bearings and the horizon; we don't know what is up and what is down. We no longer know, nor can we, what is good and evil. The tablets of the old values have been smashed. But in an earlier chapter of the same work Nietzsche perceives the death of God as an enormous opportunity: now we can set sail freely on the open sea.

The void demands to be filled; the empty throne beckons and invites new candidates to take up the mantle of the old God. Nietzsche introduces one of them: superman. The point is that the death of God also represents the death of man, the end of the existing type of humanity and humankind. A new human must come—a new God or a new "God-Man"?

Nietzsche is amazed that no new god has arrived after so long. The death of God—as another of his texts suggests—could only mean that "God has shed his moral clothes." Maybe we shall see Him once again, Nietzsche prophesies—this time beyond good and evil. Will Nietzsche ever see his god "that could dance"?

⌇

During the period since Nietzsche's death on the very threshold of the twentieth century, many "new gods" have made their appearance and there have been many attempts to present a "new man" or superman. One might even say that the century in which atheism and religious apathy—in a large part of Europe, at least—spread as never before, was also a period when "new gods" and various versions of a "new man" were mass-produced. I don't think Nietzsche would have said to any of them in a joyful spirit, in the words of his compatriot Goethe, *"Verweile doch, du bist so schön."*[6]

I wonder whether, even at this time of flourishing religion and the "return of God" to the great home of our civilization, which is the subject of so much discussion, whether it is not the return of the old destructive gods or cheap imitations of religion. What I value about our epoch is more its thirst than the beverages that it often tries to slake it with, its questions more than the answers that tend to be proposed. Aren't they above all the old *familiar* gods that are again in play?

If I had to address Zacchaeus today, I would once more seek with him the "altar to an unknown god." I would tend to seek him in a space cleansed by the process of secularization and religious critiques of recent times, rather than in today's bustling, motley, religious marketplace. And I would not be able to say anything other at that altar than what Paul proclaimed—maybe in slightly different words—in Athens long ago. That unknown god is unknown to us because we don't look for him in the right places. We seek him among the gods of this world, among philosophical constructs, projections of our own desires and fears, among "supernatural beings" and fruits of our imagination. We seek him among the ancient gods "behind the scenes" of the world in some heavenly managerial office of our destinies. We seek him like the deists of early modern times in some engineering shop for the manufacture or repair of the cosmos. But he is not anywhere there. We can't see him because he is too close. He is not a being far above us; he is the depths of our life, he is in our being, "we live, breathe, move and are in him." Things that are very close to us are easy to overlook. But he is not "close" to us, he is the closeness itself. We can still see close objects, but we can't see closeness itself. We see objects in light—we do not see the light itself. If we don't even see our own faces, but only see their reverse reflection in a mirror, as was noted earlier, how could we possibly see the face of God?

And then—like Paul at the Areopagus—I would try to show that "God's face" is only accessible to us in mirrors and riddles. It is visible in the *mirror of Easter,* in the story of Jesus of Nazareth, in that great riddle that was set for us all. Would Zacchaeus have greater patience to follow the story to the end than the citizens of Athens at the Areopagus that time? That is the question.

༈

CHAPTER 8

The Easter Mirror

The man on the road to Damascus, who heard a voice from above calling him by name, saying: "Saul, Saul why do you persecute me?" was indeed an odd apostle, not only because of the story of his dramatic conversion or because he was so strikingly different from the Twelve in terms of intelligence, character, and education. Without Paul's letters, the New Testament would have differed little from the apocalyptic literature of the day in terms of its language and the ideas it embodied. In contrast with the pitiful Greek of the synoptic Gospels and Revelation, Paul's letters contain an incredible wealth of metaphor and rhetoric, parts of which, according to the poet Henry Bauchau, are akin to the scintillating pyrotechnics of Shakespeare's plays. The linguistic style is overshadowed, however, by the style and radical character of their thinking. Without Paul, Christianity would most likely have remained one of many sects within Judaism. It is only with the arrival of Paul that it first not only transcends the cultural and religious boundaries of Israel, but also demolishes all the thitherto sacrosanct boundaries of the society of the day: it no longer mattered whether someone was Jew or pagan, man or woman, slave or free. All those barriers were relativized by what

Paul regarded as absolute: *newness* of life in Christ—the achievement of *freedom* to which we are all called, for which we have been liberated by Christ and which we must defend at all costs.[1]

It is remarkable how Paul's message was so profoundly misunderstood and his meaning and significance so totally distorted by a thinker of such genius as Nietzsche. His *Antichrist* is an aggressively hateful pamphlet, an act of provocation, a gauntlet tossed down— and Nietzsche, although he would certainly not have admitted the fact, was waiting to see who would pick it up, and in what manner. I can't help it, the author of *Antichrist* strikes me like a truculent child, whose provocatively obnoxious behavior is intended to win him assurance that he is loved. Nietzsche's renowned hammer—for his pretentiously proclaimed "hammer philosophy"—tends not to be an instrument of destruction, but rather a mineralogist's hammer investigating the hidden core of a stone, or a neurologist's hammer for testing our reflexes. If it destroys, then it does so only in order to excavate a new road or carve a pristine block of stone—to release from within it the already anticipated sculpture, a new shape, a new quality. Even amid the aggressive tirades of *Antichrist,* his sharpest and most unjust polemic with Christianity, there gushes forth at one point the most astonishing hymn of love for Jesus, bearing witness to his insightful grasp of Jesus's originality.

Nietzsche is not capable or willing to do anything similar as far as Paul is concerned. For him he has nothing but virulent words of hatred and absolute condemnation. If we compare Nietzsche's portrait of Paul and his interpretation and assessment of Paul's teachings with Paul's actual texts, the gulf could not be wider. Where did all that anger come from? Aren't the two of them in fact much more similar in many ways? Does Nietzsche, who desires to shake up

Christianity in a radical fashion, suspect that it was precisely Paul who was responsible for the enormous transformation and reinterpretation of what Christianity was "disposed" toward at the very beginning of its history, by those who feared to complete Jesus's rift with the world of Mosaic Law, or that Paul's historic victory over Peter and the other apostles at the assembly in Jerusalem—also due certainly to Peter's generous readiness for compromise—allowed the spark of Christianity's liberating radicalism to flare up into a fire that engulfed and transformed the entire civilization of the ancient world and very quickly penetrated beyond its borders?

Dietrich von Hildebrand wrote that "Nietzsche is a radically Protestant preacher." However, it was Paul who stood at the cradle of almost all the radical reformations of Christianity, from Marcion to Martin Luther, and right up to today's postmodern interpreters of Christianity (including the interpretation of secularization as a fulfillment of kenosis, self-emptying—i.e., Paul's interpretation of the meaning of Christ's cross—in the work of Gianno Vattimo). Marcion, that "first Protestant" on the threshold of the history of Christian thought, drew out and extrapolated Paul's contraposition of the Law and grace into his doctrine of two gods: the dark God— the Creator of the old Law—and Jesus's merciful Father of the Gospels. With his rejection of the old God (and the vague promise of a return of God, who would "slough off his moral skin"), isn't Nietzsche a "radical Protestant" in a certain sense, particularly in the way that he carries that attempt at liberation from the old religion, which started with Paul and Marcion, beyond the furthest bounds imaginable? With his rejection of the *bad* God, isn't Marcion the "first Nietzsche" of the church and Nietzsche, with his message of the death of the old God, "the last Marcion of Christianity"?

In his remarkable book on Paul,[2] Alain Badiou maintains that Nietzsche senses in Paul a rival rather than an enemy. After all, both of them want to initiate a new historical era, both of them are convinced that modern man is something that must be surpassed, both of them want to end the rule of guilt and law, both of them practice an "antiphilosophy," both of them want to prepare a life-affirmation event and the liberation of life from the rule of negativity and death. According to Badiou, in *The Antichrist* Nietzsche totally caricatured Paul's doctrine and his role, but one of his perceptions was correct: Jesus's entire life is of no interest to Paul; all Paul needed "was the death on the cross, *and* something more."[3] But that "something more," that "something" that conquers death, was precisely what was pivotal for Paul.

Yes, one may agree that Paul totally ignores Jesus's teaching and pays practically no attention to his preaching, his miracles, or his life as a whole as described in the Gospels—with one exception: the Easter events. Paul builds his entire Gospel, all his version of Christianity, solely on Easter—the Eucharist, the cross, and the resurrection.

Paul's aforementioned sermon on the Areopagus in Athens was also leading up to a message about Easter. Paul's interpretation of the "unknown" God, a God who is nevertheless close to us beyond all thought—in whom "we live, and move and have our being"—is merely the prelude to what he was intending to say about the cross and the resurrection. But there his sermon ended, interrupted by the derision and boredom of most of his audience. Let us try to work forward from that particular moment.

སྙ

I've already mentioned Moingt's observation that the hellenization of Christianity helped carry the Gospel into a great and influential culture but eventually resulted in a certain "re-Judaization of Christianity," because Paul's overture to all, regardless of frontiers, acted as a brake for a long time, by binding it fatefully to a single type of language and thinking. I tend to think that the "re-Judaization of Christianity" occurred when the *Roman sense* of law and morality prevailed over a certain trend of Greek patristics, Platonism and Neoplatonism inspired by Christian philosophy and philosophical mysticism—whose finest flowering was probably the "negative theology" of Gregory of Nyssa and Dionysius the Areopagite.

Judaism and Islam (which resembles it to a great extent) are essentially *legal systems,* based on the logic of the contractual relationship.[4] Jesus—and Paul even more radically so—brought about an amazing breakthrough and transformation: the attempt to *replace the "debit-credit"* relationship with a *dialectics of grace and faith,* to replace the religion of rules with a religion of love.

By a series of Old Testament covenants—and above all the covenant on Sinai—God binds Israel *and Himself.* This is certainly an incredible step, whereby God is transformed from an "unpredictable desert demon" of the ancient Orient or an "absolute ruler" into a "constitutional monarch" (to borrow the psychoanalytical language of Freud and Fromm)—and the religious relationship is now logical and transparent, like any good legal code. But Christianity takes a further and even more radical step (which is only hinted at in some themes in the Hebrew Bible and later Judaism, particularly Jewish mysticism). Jesus concludes a *new covenant* that is no longer based on law, but on love. *Love each other as I have loved you*—that is Jesus's only "commandment," and it departs entirely from the system of commandments and proscriptions strictly dividing the "clean" from the "unclean." Jesus—and, in his footsteps, even more radically, Paul—stands the entire system on its head and delegalizes religion as a whole. This was correctly understood by Jesus's opponents among the Pharisees and by Paul's opponents among Jesus's apostles and disciples.

However, God's love is "nontransparent" and "irrational" because it transcends the logic of law. It is "folly" and cannot be understood by means of "reason," but *only by love in its turn*. It cannot be fettered by a well-thought-out system of rules. It can only be expressed—using the only commandment Jesus gave his apostles at the Last Supper. Reason (and specifically the reason of religious legalism) is not "compatible with God." Only love, which is itself *charisma*, a gift of grace, is compatible with Love. *Legal reason considers it "folly."*

Yes, people have a constant desire to understand God, to grasp Him, to uncover His mystery, and they rightly sense that they will only manage it if they will be in some sense *like God*. However, there exist *two radically different paths to being like God*: the *"path of getting to know God"* (in the sense of removing the veil of His mystery and acquiring the certainty of knowledge, so that one may decide oneself what is good and evil), or the *"path of being like God"*—by imitating, through one's actions, the foolish logic of love, which is full of paradoxes. The first was the one that Satan proposed to Adam in the Garden of Eden (you will be like gods who know what is good and what is bad), the second is proposed by Jesus (be like my Father in Heaven who lets His sun shine and the rain fall on the just and the unjust). That second path—the "foolish" one—because it could scarcely have finished otherwise than on the

cross—is well understood by Paul, who radicalizes it: let us be foolish in Christ—God's foolish cause is stronger than people.

Even in the church one still encounters attempts to understand
God by hemming knowledge about Him into dogmatic definitions
and binding our relationship with Him into the straitjacket of a legal system. In place of the dramatic stories of scripture that are an
ongoing challenge for renewed reflection and inspiration for original acts of foolish love (such as those of Francis of Assisi), what is
proposed—in the form of catechisms and logically arranged dogmatic textbooks—is a well-organized timetable, which we must observe in a disciplined fashion and above all *invariably* in order to
avoid collisions. In contraposition to this are the theologians, mystics, and saints, who demonstrate that God is indefinable mystery
and that following Christ and fulfilling God's will as was illustrated
in Christ is not a matter of observing a system of commandments
and proscriptions but of the foolishness of love. And they, of course,
"collide," as Jesus did, with the defenders of the Law and as Paul
did with the founding generation of Christian conservatives and
Pharisees.

In short, God's logic is different from human logic, and people
have to experience it as paradox—and paradoxes abound in Jesus's
parables and Paul's theology of the cross, faith, and grace. The first
will be last and last first; whoever loses his life will find it; to anyone who has, more will be given, and from anyone who has not,
even what he has will be taken away; it is more blessed to give than
to receive; blessed are the poor—woe to the rich; blessed are they
who mourn; woe to you who laugh now; blessed are they who are
persecuted . . . The two mysteries at the heart of Christian theology,
Incarnation and Redemption; God in the manger and God on

the gallows, are the first and foremost of those paradoxes. That was well understood by people such as Pascal, Luther, Kierkegaard, and Bonhoeffer.

But there were also many who found the wide-open door of love and the spirit that wafted through it too risky, and they slowly started to close it by means of legal thinking. The same brilliant Anselm of Canterbury, who devised the ingenious "ontological proof of God's existence" (which, unlike all the other "proofs" is still worth reflecting on and interpreting), came up with the perverse—and, centuries later, still very influential—"satisfaction soteriology" that regards Christ's death as just payment in the oddest commercial deals between the devil, God, and man, as "compensation," settling debts and placating the pique of an aggrieved ruler.

Paul, Paul, why do we Christians still persecute you and Christ's spirit of freedom in you?

In 2007, the year in which I am writing this book, Pope Benedict XVI has proclaimed a "year of St Paul." What can we expect to happen during it?

Earlier this year, the same pope gave a brilliant lecture at the University of Regensburg that achieved instant fame as a result of the infuriated response of a large part of the Muslim world, caused by typically sensationalist reporting of the text by the mass media. I have been trying to understand why, in that lecture, Pope Benedict took issue so strongly with the tradition of the mystics and theologians who assert an incomprehensible God—a tradition that is in many ways close and dear to me.

In the face of latter-day irrationalism, postmodernist relativism, religious fundamentalism, the "cynical reason" of the pragmatics, and the narrow rationality of positivists and proponents of scientism, Benedict is calling for a *new alliance* of faith and rationalism, religion and science. He admires the patristic and scholastic marriage of the divine Logos—which is lyrically presented in the prologue to John's Gospel—and the *logos* of Hellenistic philosophy. He upholds the idea, advanced by the Emperor Michael against Islam, that God also binds Himself by ethical rules.

In his Regensburg lecture, the Pope put forward yet another fundamental argument of importance: an incomprehensible God can be dangerous—a "rational God" (unlike a hidden, mysterious, and unpredictable God) is a God who enables tolerance and dialogue. Those who profess a God in the darkness of mystery might give rise to fears that they could unleash irrational violence in the name of that God. I have given much thought to that argument, which sounds logical and consistent from the lips of a man who feels global pastoral responsibility in this era of "terror in God's name."

A number of counter questions suggest themselves. Did not those who bound God to the rationality of this world advance many sophisticated justifications of violence? Has not the rational, logically formulated theory of just war legitimized many dreadful and sinister deeds? Isn't there a need for the *new* alliance of reason and faith, which Pope Benedict calls for—no doubt rightfully and timely—to be truly *new* and not simply an artfully patched up version of the old one, which has now definitely come to grief? Does it not also call for a rethinking of the relationship between faith and reason, and also a rethinking of the very concept of rationality and the concept of faith?

Of course the God of paradoxes that Jesus and Paul presented as an alternative to the God of the Law and its rationality is not an arbitrary desert demon in whose name a holy war might be waged. His "irrationality" resides solely in the degree of "foolish" (unmerited) love and abundant grace that surpasses and overturns our rational calculations—so that with our sense of justice according to the Law we often find ourselves in the position of the aggrieved, injured, and confused elder brother from the parable of the "prodigal son," or of the laborer who endured the drudgery and heat of the day and "rightly" objected to the fact that the laborers hired for the final hours of the day received the same decent payment.

"Nor are your ways my ways. . . . As high as the heavens are above the earth, so high are my ways above your ways and my thoughts above your thoughts," we read in scripture.[5] The reason that God surpasses our legalistic thinking and our calculations of justice according to the "credit-debit" model is the magnanimity of His boundless love—and that is demonstrated most eloquently in the paradox of the Easter story.

ॐ

I have suggested that God *is unknown because He is so close.* Generally we are unaware of the air we breathe. We do not see the light itself, only things in the light. We don't even see our own face—only its reflection in the mirror. Likewise we can only see God's face in a mirror—and that mirror, says Paul, is Jesus, or rather His Easter story. Paul wants to know nothing except *Jesus crucified.*[6] As was pointed out earlier, Paul "does not know" (or at least he never refers to) Jesus in the manger, in the desert, or on Mount Tabor, let alone

Jesus preaching, healing, changing water into wine at Cana, multiplying loaves near Capharnaum, praying on the Mount of Olives, or walking on water.

The landscape of Paul's thinking is dominated by the cross—even to the extent that the very message of the Resurrection, which I'm sure we would identify as the core of the Easter message, sometimes seems "overshadowed *by the cross.*" The cross and Resurrection are undoubtedly indissolubly coupled in the Christian Gospel. Their relationship is not always symmetrical, however. Whereas "without the cross" (and everything the cross means—including Jesus's abandonment by the Father) the news of the Resurrection would actually be, in a sense, *dangerous,* the cross, in a certain sense, constitutes a victory, which is then proclaimed by the "morning after the Sabbath," the empty tomb, and what we hear about it from the angel seated on the displaced stone. What would be "dangerous" about the news of the Resurrection *detached* from the Easter story was explained succinctly by J. B. Metz: if the cry of the Crucified One is not heard in our preaching about the Resurrection, then our message is the mythology of victory, not the core of Christian theology. (In my view, the Hollywood-style spectacular portrayal of the Passion in Mel Gibson's recent film *The Passion of the Christ* was a telling illustration of that—essentially unchristian—"mythology of victory".)[7]

Paul is passionately concerned that "the cross of Christ might not be emptied of its meaning" (1 Cor. 1:17). We should also be concerned that that message should not be emptied of meaning and diluted by anything—even a superficial understanding of the Resurrection. When I sketched some ideas along these lines in one of my books, a reviewer in some Lefebvrist journal made the bald claim that I do not believe in the Resurrection (with the additional charming comment that "he is not even a heretic anymore, because he is no longer a Christian"). How wrong they are! My concern is to protect the profound truth of the Resurrection from being dumbed down, to prevent it too from being "emptied of meaning" and being diminished by our locating it among the *bruta facta*—the everyday events of our world. It is neither an everyday event nor a "miracle" of the kind we read about in the Gospel story, whether it be the changing of water into wine at Cana or the resuscitation of Lazarus. It is something incomparably greater and more important—it cannot be compared to anything else.

That is why the Resurrection message requires from us *much more than our intellectual assent*—because when it is forced to gaze into the abyss of that mystery our intellect naturally suffers vertigo. It demands from us a still deeper involvement, something much more fundamental: *our existential acceptance of that event,* with this great truth of faith. *To believe in Christ's Resurrection* means something else, something much more than simply accepting a particular theory or espousing the opinion that *it once happened.* Our belief in the Resurrection is confirmed by our *involvement in that event, by our joint resurrection.* According to Paul, we have already been raised with Christ (Col. 3:1)—and since Christ rose from the dead, we too must now live in newness of life![8]

When, on Good Friday, I read the Passion according to John, which ends with the sealing of the tomb, or when I am walking the Stations of the Cross, which culminates with that same event, the placing of Jesus in the tomb, what I am conscious of always is that the tomb is ourselves. *The Resurrection is to take place within ourselves.*

The fact that the central symbol of Christianity is the cross and not a representation of the Resurrection is not, of course, because the Resurrection and the resurrected Jesus would be trickier to portray artistically. The crosses on the walls of our churches and our homes challenge us to go and narrate the story's continuation *by how we live!* The last station of the cross is the depiction of the entombment, but the contemplative journey must be continued along our own life's path. We are told: Now you have been chosen as a "witness of the Resurrection"—it is now for you to bear witness to the way Jesus is present in this world and how he is alive in these days!

I insist that belief in the Resurrection and Christians' readiness to bear witness to Christ's presence and vitality draws strength from *the event* of the Resurrection and not simply from the inspirational power of some mythological image. I believe that the presence of the Resurrected One in our world is fundamentally *more real* than the presence of the *ever-living ideas* of one or other of the gallery of "the great departed." I would even go so far as to say that the reality of the Resurrection forces me to revise my previously over-narrow understanding of reality and breaks through the horizon of the world of my experience into the depths of bottomless mystery. And not just my *understanding of reality,* but the very reality of my life, and my life itself thereby acquires a new depth and a new meaning—and that meaning is already present in my life—even though it has not yet in fact transformed it—at least as a call, as *an invitation into the depths,* which I can either accept or reject.

I believe with Paul that if Christ did not rise from the dead our faith is in vain (1 Cor. 15:17)—but equally vain, pointless, and empty would our belief in Resurrection be if it simply remained nothing more than an opinion or conviction and had no influence on our lives, if we too were not resurrected to a new life. If, according to Paul, our belief in Jesus's resurrection is the condition of our salvation, then that belief must clearly be something *much more* than our conviction that *it once happened*; after all, our opinions and suppositions, the theories we agree with, and the knowledge we carry in our heads are not what is going to save us. The *cause* of our redemption was Christ's sacrifice on the cross—and we accept (embrace) that unmerited gift of grace through faith. That faith, however, means allowing that event to enter our lives as a whole as a transforming power; it is not enough simply to include it among our knowledge about famous events of the distant past.

Belief in the Resurrection means accepting that "strength that showed itself in weakness," the strength of Christ's sacrifice—His sacrificial *love* as a living reality. Not to believe in Christ's Resurrection is to live as if the cross were the final end, as if Christ's life and His sacrifice were a hopeless fiasco, a pointless, absurd defeat, something that can never inspire anymore. To live that way would amount to "emptying Christ's cross of meaning," not accepting the proffered grace, "not to believe in the Resurrection," and to close oneself off from salvation. It would amount to "remaining in the tomb"—and now, in this present life, not entering into the newness and fullness of life that Christ opened up with his victory over death—and to probably lose the hope that nothing can exclude me from that new ("eternal") life apart from my sin, apart from my free refusal. Its darkest consequence would be to lose hope that not even the death of my body can destroy that "newness."

Even those who "for no fault of their own did not receive Christ"—either because they lived before Him or because the Gospel tidings never reached their ears, *or because the message came in such a form that they could not accept it in all good conscience or in the light of their understanding*—can, as the Catholic Church now teaches, nevertheless be saved, if they have lived according to their conscience and understanding. These people participate in the Incarnation event—the "Christmas mystery"—by virtue of their very humanity, so long as they accept it as a "gift and task" and strive to fulfill that assignment conscientiously and faithfully. And they plainly share in the Easter mystery insofar as they cherish within their lives the same sacrificing love that led right to the cross, insofar as they try to overcome their own selfishness, and insofar as they do not accept as final the setbacks that that love encounters in the course of their lives. Christ's victory over death is truly an event of a special kind and not "just another event." What distinguishes it from the other historical facts is that it is "visible" solely with the *eyes of faith*—and because in the here and now even faith sees all the things of God *only partially and as in a mirror*, it must be supported in the darkness of our lives by *patience* and the perseverance of hope.

Christ's Resurrection must remain a provocation, *foolishness* in the eyes of "the wisdom of the world." It must remain a "scandal" for those who don't share the faith, or also for the "unbeliever within us"—as Paul writes.[9] If we sought to "prove" that central mystery of our faith (such as by means of rational theology), and make it something that could be painlessly and easily acceptable for all, even the "wise and cautious" of the world, we would *empty* it.

No human experience, reason, or senses could roll away by themselves the stone that conceals the mystery of the Resurrection—faith alone, supported by hope and love, can hear the message of the Resurrection. That event is hidden, unseen. In the hymn *"Exultet,"* we sing that only the night knew when it happened—but in the midst of history it should be present through the testimony of those who make known that Christ is not a finished chapter.

ᢌ

I have said a lot about God's hiddenness, silence, and remoteness. It is necessary to add that God does reveal Himself, of course. And the core of our faith is that His fullest self-expression, His Word, which He gave us and will never take back, the Word whereby He speaks to us and which He shares with us, is Jesus's humanity. Jesus is the best real symbol and forceful sign of God's presence for us and among us. *He is the window through which we view God at work.* He is the face of the invisible and the name of the unnameable. His life on earth is the sun that peeped out of the impenetrable clouds. However, for our faith and our salvation that event is a sufficient act of God's proximity.

But the dialectics of God's concealment and disclosure apply even here. Here on earth Jesus was for those around Him a multivalent phenomenon, and family ties and family clans were divided according to how He was received and understood. Even in Him—as Kierkegaard observed—God did not discard His incognito. And it had scarcely begun to become *clear* to His closest and most devoted followers, His Twelve, when God started to toss their certainties about like a fishing boat in a gale—God hid His face "in the darkness at noon," in the dark shadow of Good Friday.

And what came next? What remained for the apostles "on this side of history" in terms of tangible, visible, and verifiable things was the *empty tomb*—and a whole range of possible interpretations open to believers and unbelievers alike.[10] And then the reality of their lives starts to be penetrated by things that can also be "touched"—signs, traces of the Crucified One. However, the healing way that these "things" (such as the bread of the Emmaus supper and Christ's wounds, bared for Thomas) can be touched is faith.

We too have Christ's bread and the wine of his blood "available" to us on our altars. We too can touch his wounds in the unhealed scars on the bodies and souls of our suffering neighbors. And even though those remarkable forty days after the Crucifixion are sealed by the event of the Ascension, nevertheless the great gifts of Easter, those traces of the Crucified One, remain among us here on earth. After all, during the Ascension, didn't the angels tell Christ's disciples (and us too, therefore) to stop fixing their gaze on "the sky" and shift it back to the earth? "Men of Galilee, why are you standing there looking at the sky?"—that angelic rebuke is addressed to us as well, if we ignore Christ's everyday presence in our world (a presence concealed in the everyday). It is always necessary to come down from the mount of the Ascension, as also from the clear light of Mount Tabor into the valley, sometimes even into the "valley of shadows," and even into the darkness of Gethsemane. Radiance and shadow alternate in the life of every true disciple of Christ, just as they do in the history of the church—just as they did in Christ's life on earth. But how are we to look from that dim light at the event of the Resurrection, which we are told is the cornerstone of Christian belief?

The mystery of Christ's Resurrection does not confront us like a detective problem that we could solve by verifying one of several hypotheses. Nor is it a fact of nature or history that we might discover, describe, and explain using scientific methods (and I am unable to trust those theologies that pretend to do so—by pinning their hopes on traditional dogmatic concepts or on "demytholo-gization" of some kind). It confronts us more as a sort of *koan,* a rid-dle defying the powers of reason and yielding its meaning only in the flash of a spark that leaps, spontaneous and unforeseeable, be-tween God and us—from God's side the spark is called grace and from ours it is called faith.

Resurrection—from God's viewpoint—is a perfect and com-pleted action, whereby the Father freed the Son from the snares of death. Seen (imperfectly, how else?) from the viewpoint of the his-tory of the church and world, however, that event is still an "un-finished revolution"—it is like a subterranean river, boring its way through the hard soil of our lack of faith, sinfulness, and closed-mindedness, and only here and there visibly gushing out amid the incidents of our lives. When Mary Magdalene heard her name from the lips of the one she took to be the gardener, when Paul on the road to Damascus heard the question "Saul, Saul, why are you per-secuting me?" and when St. Augustine in the garden heard the song "Tole, lege!" these were not simply post-Resurrection events; the power and the reality of the Resurrection was *within* those events. The Resurrection *happened* there too, so that those people were able to experience it as an unfinished, living event. We also *shall be united with him in the resurrection* (Rom. 6:5).

And weren't many of Jesus's deeds here on earth, whether the marriage at Cana, the call to Zacchaeus, or the raising of Lazarus, a kind of "anticipation of the Resurrection"? God's actions embrace all dimensions of human time, and even though they occurred uniquely and irrevocably at one particular historical moment, the way for them is always paved by their "prototypes" and they die away and return into the present as anamnesis, "recollection"—not only perhaps in liturgical events, but also in the testimonies of the saints (including those not canonized). They are the past, insofar as they are the *intentions* of recollection, but the very *"act"* of recollection makes them present, we are present in the present, and the past event "catches up with us" and now proceeds with our time (is contemporary). And if these great deeds of God's "operate in history," above all secretly or "incognito"—to use Kierkegaard's favorite expression—they are, however, preparing the moment when they will be revealed to all of us in the total manifestation of their meaning—"at the end of time."

Many distinguished theologians support the theory of *"creatio continua"*—continuing creation; could we not similarly speak of a *"ressurectio continua,"* a continuing Resurrection?

Augustine wrote somewhere that praying means to close one's eyes and realize that God is creating the world *now.* I would add: to believe means to open one's heart and realize that *now, at this very moment* the sealed stone has been rolled aside and the rays of the Easter morning have triumphed over the cold, dark tomb.

૱

CHAPTER 9

A Time to Gather Stones

The time of human life is not a time of things, it is not simply *chronos*—time flowing onward in one direction like water in a river, the time of clocks and calendars. It is also *kairos*—the time of opportunity, a time that is ripe, *a time for something.* "There is an appointed time for everything, and a time for every affair under the heavens," we read in the book of Ecclesiastes. "A time to be born, and a time to die; a time to plant, and a time to uproot the plant. A time to kill, and a time to heal; a time to tear down, and a time to build. A time to weep, and a time to laugh; a time to mourn, and a time to dance. A time to scatter stones, and a time to gather them."[1]

What sort of time is now, as the Zacchaeuses of today wait to be called upon? What is today's time for? What can we learn from the signs of the time that Jesus, like the prophets, invited his listeners to read? It is a time for *gathering stones*, for clearing them away. There has been enough stone throwing. It is a *time for closeness.*

૱

"Technology has overcome all distances but has created no closeness," wrote Martin Heidegger. I have often recalled that sentence when changing planes at international airports, which, like hotel rooms in different countries and on different continents, start to resemble one another like peas in a pod.

After the end of Communist rule, during which, for twenty years, I was not allowed to travel beyond the frontiers of my country, or rather, outside the borders of the "socialist camp," the new gates of opportunity were suddenly thrown open to me. The world of distances suddenly invaded my life, and although I had just reached the age of forty, I was so enraptured by its scents, colors, and melodies that I had the impression of being borne back across the "lost years" and regaining my youth. I drank thirstily and with feverish enthusiasm from that magically bubbling fountain of new opportunities.

After several lectures in various European countries, invitations started to pile up on my desk and in my Internet mailbox (it was the period when I first discovered the world of computers) for me to give speeches, lectures, and seminars at universities and congresses in various parts of the world. During those first years I accepted them almost indiscriminately. Visits to several European countries were followed by my first trip to the USA, where I traveled round a number of states, lecturing at a dozen universities and colleges (I subsequently returned to America again and again). I lectured in Chile, Argentina, India, Canada, and the Chinese Republic of Taiwan. Lectures, study trips, and meetings in the framework of interfaith dialogue, and then collaboration on a multiserial TV program on the five most widespread world religions took me to Israel and Egypt, Morocco, Japan, Nepal, Thailand, Burma, Australia, and many other places. And when, after that welter of words in various corners of the world, I felt an urgent need for silence, I traveled to be quiet to the scorching deserts of Egypt and the freezing ice floes of the Antarctic.[2]

At the very end of the twentieth century and in the first years of the new millennium, I spent an incredible amount of time on board airplanes. I was handed my gins and tonic by air hostesses with white, black, and yellow skins, and on those flights I read possibly more books than before my final examinations at university. Globalization, the process of growing together and its upshot in the field of religion, was often touched on in my lectures, and I literally felt the effects of it on my own—by then understandably wearier and wearier—body. The world started to look small to us, albeit even less transparent. There are no distant destinations anymore. But Heidegger is right: overcoming distances doesn't necessarily mean finding closeness.

Creating closeness—that is a spiritual task that we cannot delegate to any technical instrument of our expansion, our domination of the world. How is closeness created? This question is simply a variation of the one put to Jesus by the Pharisees: who is my neighbor? The answer is the same: make yourself a neighbor!

ॐ

The time for creating closeness is "the time to gather stones together." Our entire world is strewn with stones that are heavy, sharp, and dangerous, because they solicit us—again and again—to use them to stone others with. Old quarrels, misunderstandings that have never been cleared up, frustrations, mutual disappointments, trespasses unforgiven—they can all harden into stone. Everything can be transformed into boulders of prejudice and animosity blocking paths between people, nations, cultures, and religions. Let us at last end the murderous time of "casting stones," let us remove these stones from the landscape of our "shrinking world"! The bringer of salvation cannot come to the many waiting Zacchaeuses of today while these boulders continue to bar the way. It is a very urgent task.

It was on that very road between Jerusalem and Jericho, at the border crossing between Israeli and Palestinian territory in the Holy Land, at a place of roadblocks and threateningly bristling weapons, that the question occurred to me: could Jesus today enter those places where His conversation with Zacchaeus occurred two thousand years ago? It is not foliage that obscures the view of today's Zacchaeuses but a rampart of weapons, wrongs, and hate. These days it is hard not to be aware of this atmosphere in Jericho, in the same way that I had sensed it earlier in Hebron at the graves of the patriarchs bespattered several years ago by the blood of praying Muslims, shot by the weapon of a Jewish fanatic. How many victims have since been claimed by the violence of extremists from the other side and by the conflict among Palestinians themselves? Is it possible through this rampart of hatred to glimpse "the feet of Him who brings glad tidings"?[3]

Isn't Jesus's invitation, His words telling us He wants to be near to us and enter our home—not only in the Holy Land, not only in Jericho, but in many places of our planet, which is so densely interlinked—drowned out by the din of voices that have gradually erased the word "peace" from their vocabulary? And when they do talk about it, they do nothing or not enough to offer a truly radical alternative to the "spirit of revenge" and violence of our world. Where are the *peacemakers* that Jesus names in His eight beatitudes?

჻

Of course, Jesus also says, "I come to bring not peace but the sword" (Matt. 10:34). However, one would have to be extremely blind of heart and determined not to understand, if one were to misinterpret this sentence as a "killing word" justifying violence. Jesus isn't talking here about a sword that He or His supporters should or have the right to use against their enemies, but one that would *strike Him and His disciples.*[4] After all, Christ comes as a "sign that will be contradicted"—and scarcely has old Simeon pronounced this prophecy over the child Jesus than he says to the child's mother: "and you yourself a sword will pierce" (Luke 2:35). "Put your sword back into its sheath," Jesus says to Peter, when the apostle goes to defend Him.[5] And before His death, when He prophesies a time of swords, the apostles reply that they have two swords. Jesus's response, "It is enough!" (i.e., that's more than enough), is proof that his previous sentence truly cannot be interpreted as a call for them to arm themselves and rely on force. The fundamental characteristic that distinguishes "His Kingdom" (i.e., His style of "government") from the powers of this world is a consistent rejection of violence: "If my kingdom did belong to this world, my attendants (would) be fighting," Jesus says to Pilate.[6]

Nevertheless—and maybe for that very reason—His coming into the world brings the *sword of division.* Old Simeon prophesied about Him that He was "destined for the fall and rise of many in Israel" (Luke 2:34). Willy-nilly, His arrival gives rise to two camps: the camp of His supporters and the camp of His opponents, and the frontier between them will cut through nations, tribes, and families: "one's enemies will be those of his household."[7] The radical arrival of good naturally radicalizes evil also. Jesus knows that the sword of persecution will never be far from Him and those loyal to Him—they bring it with them, not as a weapon but in the way that light brings a shadow in its train. Only in pitch darkness are there no shadows. Only the devil, according to old interpretations, has no shadow, because he is shadow itself.

The shadow of violence will continue to fall across our world in various forms—this is something to reckon with. But reckoning with it does not mean being resigned to it, let alone deserting to the camp of violence or imitating its methods, allowing oneself to be overpowered by its spirit, and "playing a hand dealt by evil." What Jesus says about stumbling blocks to faith applies equally to violence—and violence is and remains a stumbling block, a disgrace of our world: "Things that cause sin will inevitably occur, but woe to the person through whom they occur."[8]

꒛

The world was confronted afresh with that great theme of the Gospels on September 11, 2001, a date that has become a symbol of a new type of violence in our world. The very concept of terror—an unscrupulously declared program of using violence systematically as the state's main political tool for mass intimidation of "the enemies within" and total control of citizens—was the child of the French Revolution, which launched the modern era beneath the banner of freedom, equality, and brotherhood. However, present-day terrorism represents further "progress" in the history of violence—and it relies chiefly on the power of the mass media. Without their influence it would not be effective enough.

The planners of the September 11 attack needed *TV images* of the collapsing skyscrapers that would circle the globe in an instant far more than they needed the actual dead bodies. Those pictures, not the explosives, represent the main strength and power of terrorism; chemical explosives are simply an essential preparatory agent—the main weapons are the explosive *images*. The emotions aroused by these images are the main objective of the terrorists; killing is simply a by-product. After all, the terrorists are not concerned about these people or their deaths, but instead about the psychological effect their deaths will achieve by means of media images. Without those images the attacks themselves would be a marginal, localized affair. There have been countless wars in history, as well as the extermination of enormous numbers of people—and in that context, however cynical it may sound, September 11 was an utterly marginal phenomenon. However, the triumph of violence is that it can become visible in this way and virtually enter the homes of billions of people on all continents, and spread fear, as it is intended to.

In several of my most recent books and in many lectures, I have developed the idea that *the media are the religion of the Western world today* (whereas since the Enlightenment, modern Christianity has lost the character of a "religion" in the sociological sense, in other words, of being an integrative force of society as a whole, of being its common language).[9] The mass media fulfill the main aspects of religion's social role—i.e., a force that holds society together, influencing people's style of thinking and their lifestyles, offering shared symbols and "great narratives," creating a human network, but above all *interpreting the world*. We obtain the bulk of what we know about various aspects of the world—from politics to sport—via the mass media. And even in the case of the most "objective" and serious media, that mediation is not an unadorned mirror of reality. The very mechanism whereby "subjective" reality is transformed into "objective," representative reality is itself *interpretation* (even though there need not be any deliberate intention to "distort the truth"). The media are arbiters of the truth, which is one of the basic roles of *religion*: most people regard some event as *true* because they saw it *with their own eyes* on the TV screen, and *important* because it was in the forefront of the news broadcast or on the front page of the newspaper. Avid television viewers gradually learn to let the "eyes of the camera" replace their "own eyes" to the extent that their immediate perception of things is then unwittingly influenced and structured by camera optics (and implicitly by the ideology of the mass media producers), so that they are no longer capable of looking with their own eyes and thinking with their own brains, judging things with their own conscience (and these organs of their humanity—and along with them their individuality and personal identity—gradually atrophy and die).

This religion, this sacred space of contemporary civilization, this semblance of truth—*aletheia,* "illuminated" (i.e., accessible, public) space—has been conquered by modern terrorism and turned into its most powerful weapon and the main instrument of its influence. By no means is it my intention to demonize the media—it is "in good faith" that they give so much space for news and pictures of terrorist actions. Besides, it is their duty and the whole point of their service to the public. After all, it is no one's wish to censor out bad news or close one's eyes to the tragic events of our world; we all have a sacred right to information! But that is precisely the reason that terrorism's power over the media—and, via them, over us—is so enormous and so dangerous. It is precisely this *innocence* of the media (they serve both us, who have a need for their news and demand it, and, whether they like it or not, terrorism also, which has a similar vital need of it) that represents the greatest danger, because it renders the world of the media—i.e., our most intrinsically shared world—defenseless. We are incapable of preventing this greatest success of the terrorists: the mass dissemination of fear through the media; we all contribute to it. And it is understandable. We do indeed have a sacred right to it, and we know no alternative: we cannot blind the eye whereby we perceive the world beyond our borders that is invisible to our own eyes; we quite rightly have no wish to be deaf to news about events out of earshot and thus deprive ourselves of topics that are so fresh that they have not entered our minds. Here and now, constantly and every day, the media provide us already with what St. Paul thought only heaven would offer us: "What eye has not seen, and ear has not heard, and what has not entered the human heart" (1 Cor. 2:9). The media are now our heaven and are gradually changing the face of the earth.

But one of the "incarnations" of the great symbols of that artificial heaven is precisely terrorism. In the very same way that, according to the Gospels, the preexistent Word took upon itself the form of specific historical events and entered into the material reality of our life stories, it happened—in a weird inversion—on September 11.

A woman who was a direct eyewitness of the attack on New York—that "lightning bolt out of the blue"—told me that she first thought she was in some horror film: after all, millions of Americans could have seen countless times that very scene of falling skyscrapers and been thoroughly entertained by those vivid, dramatic, and highly photogenic images. Every night they had the opportunity—and many took it—to enjoy titillation of the nerves, a pleasantly chilling sensation in their tummies, and thrills, much more cheaply than in popular adrenaline sports. Eventually some fairly exotic King Kong, some antimessiah, had to come along so that those archetypal images could be incarnated into everyday reality, so that the virtual world could burst the bounds of the TV screen and come out into the street, so that the entertainment of the night could be transformed into the horror of the day.

Each of us is familiar with nightmarish and cruel dreams that a psychoanalyst would explain as an emanation of the aggression lurking deep in each of us—shadows, he would tell us, that our culture offers various ways to integrate and sublimate, in order to evade two (in the final analysis, mutually attractive) extremes, i.e., either to force ourselves to suppress them into our unconscious and from there let them poison our lives like an untreated ulcer, or naively to let them gradually take control of our consciousness and behavior. The success of horror and action films is probably due to the fact that these very dreams—of which we usually recall only fragments, and possibly that is their fascination for us, as unfinished business or forbidden fruit in the Garden of Eden of our dream world—bring them back into our conscious, manipulate them (and us) and take them to their fantastic consequences, and make them a part of the omnipresent entertainment industry.

This toying with images from deep inside is a kind of *antimeditation*. Meditation is concerned with "achieving freedom from images," emptying the mind—whereas here it is a matter of filling the mind and controlling it by means of fascinating images (for that matter, the advertisements that pepper those films, and which are the economic motive for their distribution, operate according to that very principle). Meditation is intended to achieve spiritual freedom—this antimeditation achieves the opposite effect, one that is gladly accepted and sought after by many. Although it promises freedom in the form of escape, it is a drug that actually creates dependence and takes away people's freedom.

Could we really have thought that this trifling with powerful images from the depths of the unconscious could be kept under control forever, like those who naively think they can trifle with drugs? Did we really fail to notice that the thing that we were supposed to be playing with was more and more playing with us and dominating us? Did we really fail to suspect that these powerful images would one day break down the barriers we had established and would start to lead lives of their own? Were we really incapable of imagining how they would affect our lives? Were we really incapable of realizing that the warning voices (albeit few in number and easily ridiculed) were not calling for censorship but for culture, that it was not they who threatened freedom but the thing they were warning against?

One commentator wrote that bin Laden was nurtured not so much on the sacred texts of Islam as on Hollywood films—and he was probably right. Bin Laden is also *our shadow* and not just the shadow of Islam, and until we realize this, all the battles with terrorism will be lost in advance. I do not intend to question in a naively pacifistic way the legitimacy of any form of defense, nor blame the victim in masochistic fashion. I would be so glad if one of the *spiritual representatives of Islam* had the courage that John Paul II had when he spoke with such openness and humility, on the eve of the new millennium, about the dark aspects of the Christian past. I would love to hear from lips like his something about the extent to which bin Laden is an incarnation of the negative aspects of Islam's past. When I read thinking like this in books and articles by Salman Rushdie or in the brilliant lecture by Benedict XVI in Regensburg, these are certainly interesting and legitimate voices, but they cannot have the healing power for the spiritual world of Islam, which can only be brought about by penitent self-examination, *by a voice from inside.* Our indispensable role is to search our consciences to discover in what way our own culture might have helped bring about something that many in our environment perceive as entirely alien and incomprehensible.

॰৵৹

In our day there is one nightmarish exception to Heidegger's statement that technology has overcome all distances but failed to create any closeness. Via the media, technology has brought the horror of terrorism close to each one of us. This is, of course, *virtual* closeness, but the emotions aroused by that closeness are very real, nonetheless. If one wanted to counter the assertion that terrorism has proved victorious through its use of the media, one could certainly argue, in respect of those selfsame emotional reactions, that the images of terrorist violence have aroused in many people—with the possible exception of a few psychologically deviant individuals or ideologically blinkered groups—disapprobation and feelings of repulsion toward those actions and those who commit them.

But the terrorists neither expect nor seek our assent—they want *our fear.* They are not afraid of our rejection or our hatred. On the contrary, they welcome reactions of hatred because they rightly sense that these reactions conceal the very thing the terrorists seek to achieve: our fear. And if that mixture of fear and hatred arouses violence from our side, they are even more triumphant. They do not particularly fear military actions, because they know full well that what was designed for wars between armies does not work in campaigns against diffuse actions that tend to be organized from many epicenters of cyberspace rather than from a single bunker, against which it would be possible to send troops and declare victoriously before the camera: We got him! They are not afraid of provoking protests, defiance, and anger, because in such a climate they move about like fish in water, and far more easily than their ideological opponents. It is precisely in a biosphere of hatred that terrorists flourish best and their influence spreads like the plague.

The terrorists want the fear in our hearts to triumph. That would be their moral victory and more important to them, I am convinced, than physical domination of the globe. I don't think bin Laden is striving to sit at the table in the Oval Office of the White House and dictate sharia law to America from there. He has already won a victory when enough people are frightened at the thought of something of the kind. The terrorists are bound to have a hunch just how hard it is to rule, both physically and politically, and that it is harder than to achieve domination, even by military means. They prefer to achieve domination over the nervous system of present-day humanity, fairly easily and very quickly, by invading people's conscious and subconscious by means of suggestive images. And they are well aware that so far all our means of reacting to violence are ineffective. Neither diplomatic negotiations by statesmen (whom with?), nor protest demonstrations by pacifists (outside whose embassy?), nor military expeditions can have any effect. This new type of terrorism is a disease that cannot be eliminated by means of rapid operations—rapid operations are too risky, and they can have even more fatal consequences than the disease itself.

I don't regard myself as a pacifist, and I'm definitely not a pacifist at any price. I accept that a society has a right to defend itself by force if it is morally convinced that its vital functions or fundamental values are truly and immediately at risk, and that after all other means have been exhausted it can be sensibly assumed that only defense by force will achieve the desired effect. However, in the face of modern terrorism it is impossible rationally to assume the latter.

Madeleine Albright is right when she says that "the war with terrorism must be above all a war of ideas" and that it is a matter of demonstrating convincingly to those struggling against the secular West in the name of moral and transcendental values that not even the West intends—in spite of any "separation of state and religion"—to displace the spiritual and transcendental dimension from public life and politics, and that it takes such values seriously. Yes, this is probably the only admissible "preventive war"! However, let us admit that we have already lost a whole number of battles in that "war" in the recent period. Rabid forms of religion ought not drive our societies in the direction of rabid secularism, or of attempts to misuse our religions in a rabid manner. Maybe it's not too late to show by our example that the great values of modern times and the great values of religious faith can complement each other and mutually strengthen each other—and several commentaries by the former American secretary of state (of Czech origin) have encouraged me in that hope. Allow me to repeat yet again one of the underlying messages of the present book: my conviction that there is nothing more important in our world today than to find a path between religious fundamentalism on the one hand and fanatical secularism on the other.

٭

Could the media, which I said do so much to boost the influence and power of terrorism (albeit, I repeat, "in good faith" and, alas, unavoidably it would seem), use their powerful influence in some way to assist the spiritual battle with that evil, which is essentially also of a spiritual nature? I am convinced that in one respect they can: *by restoring the identities of the victims.* By giving them back their names and lending them a voice.

There is yet one more new and terrifying aspect of this new type of terrorism: *the blindness of the killing and the anonymity of the victims.* The terrorists don't care at all *whom* they kill. Their concern is for spectacular media footage of as many *bodies* as possible. They are most of all interested in the numbers, not the identity, of the victims. Bodies, not people.

For centuries, assassinations—unlike ordinary murders for money or out of jealousy—were targeted against specific individuals, and particularly representatives or symbols of authority. The guillotines of the French Revolution killed (real or supposed) political opponents mechanically, on a massive scale—and even more cynically than in the trials of the Spanish Inquisition—but the victims were still "selected." Hitler went one step further in the history of terrorism: he had millions of people killed without having any interest in their names, what they had done, or even their political persuasion—the only thing they had in common was that they were Jewish. But present-day terrorism does not even care in the least who its victims are—the victims have nothing in common, no common characteristic. The victims of those who destroyed the Twin Towers in New York, with Allah's name on their lips, included Jews, unbelievers, and Muslims.

If I am to be murdered, I am capable of understanding and accepting that someone might kill me for my political or religious convictions, or simply because my face doesn't fit, but it is a horrifying thought that someone might murder me simply because I am walking along Oxford Street at 10:42 on a Tuesday morning. Of course, every death—at least from the human viewpoint—is incomprehensible to a certain extent, and every violent death is somehow absurd. And even if a car happened to knock me down in Oxford Street I would probably find it somewhat absurd. But the terrorist attacks that occur nowadays, whereby anonymous victims are selected arbitrarily, combine the absurdity of an accident with the conscious and deliberate intent of a crime. The terrorists have nothing at all against the people they kill; they cannot even reproach them for wearing the uniform of a foreign army or for being citizens of a country that has officially declared war on them. Their favorite targets are international centers where there are people of all nations, races, and religions, so that the news should spread as widely as possible and affect the largest possible number of people. Not only do they not know their victims personally, they do not even meet them at the moment of death—at these executions no judge, no executioner or commanding officer is present in person, there is simply an anonymous package of explosive—or the executioners themselves voluntarily become the victims and bring down death upon their victims and themselves. The terrorists who, in this way, indiscriminately take things into their own hands and destroy their own and others' lives—like a thunderbolt from above—are, in a peculiar way, opponents of God, who—as Jesus says—allows the rain to fall and the sun to shine on the just and unjust, and on good and evil alike.

This utterly indiscriminate killing deprives the victims of *their identities* and their human dignity, as if they were gas-chamber victims stripped of their clothes. I am extremely grateful for the fact that the walls of the Pinkas Synagogue in Prague are covered in the names of the Holocaust victims and that those names are read out there for days on end, just as in many Holocaust museums around the world. In the biblical tradition, the attempt "not to erase the name" of man has a profound justification.

When I stood for the first time after the events of September 11 at "Ground Zero"—in a state of deeper emotion than I expected— I was extremely grateful for the fact that I could see there the photographs and names of the victims, that I was able, at least in this manner, to get a look at their faces.

The great Jewish thinker Emmanuel Levinas maintained that God is not revealed to human beings in any other way than *in the face of their neighbor.* The face of the other is naked and vulnerable— but that is why it is an appeal, the single real imperative that binds us with unconditional authority. It reminds us that we are called to be responsible for others, that we must assume the task that Cain rejected: to be our brothers' and sisters' keepers. The meaning of love resides precisely in responsibility. Each human being is summoned to answer for the other. That summons is our most intrinsic election—and that is true for all people. By being chosen, one is willy-nilly given responsibility for everyone and everything: "Being chosen makes one his brother's hostage." Even if we are not responsible for the evil that is done, we must not think that it does not concern us. The meaning of being chosen lies in the fact that we are responsible for the fate of the other. According to Levinas, belief in God is expressed in untiring obligations toward the other.

The theologian Johann Baptist Metz, one of the founders of liberation theology, has long asserted that the concept of *solidarity*, so crucial to Latin American theology—as well as for its Polish variation: "the theology of liberation from the Marxist regime," particularly as propounded by Józef Tischner—must be complemented by "solidarity with the victims." History is written by the victors—but the victims also remain in the memory of God. Nations and their leaders celebrate the sacrifices they have made, the victims in their own ranks. The prophetic voice of Christians should also recall the victims they have caused. And not only the voice of Christians: the British Chief Rabbi Jonathan Sacks recalls a speech given by Yitzhak Rabin, the commander in chief of the Israeli armed forces, at the Hebrew University in Jerusalem, after Israel's triumphal victory against overwhelming odds in the Six-Day War of 1967. Rabin declared that for many members of the forces their joy at victory was mixed with sadness and astonishment. Many were not even celebrating the victory because they still had in their mind's eye both their fallen comrades and the enormous losses among their enemies. It was somewhat reminiscent of the scene in the Bible when David and his entire army weep after the victory over Absalom and his warriors; Absalom was an insurgent, an enemy, but he was also David's son.

Jesus's cry on the cross, "My God, why have you forsaken me," lends a voice to all abandoned, forgotten, and silenced victims of violence. Christ, who on the cross showed unbounded solidarity— of which "solidarity with the victims" is truly part and parcel—is *our peace*; He broke down all frontiers. Efforts to revive in our consciences and in our memories the faces of victims veiled by oblivion, beyond the frontiers of "us" and "them," are part of the appeal made to us by St. Paul: *that the cross of Christ might not be emptied of its meaning.*

৵

Let us return, however, for the last time, to the major responsibility of the media. Yes, this is something at least, perhaps, that the media could do in the moral battle with terrorism: to read the names of the victims and *show their faces,* as well as tell their stories and give their loved ones a chance to speak—to summon them back from the anonymity of figures into human shape. But will they prove capable of doing it in a style that differs from the rapid succession of sensational news items? Will they prove capable of not spoiling it with sickly sentimentality or manipulation of emotions designed to use its emotional potential for ideological ends and sell it for political purposes?

When I first heard the term "war on terrorism" amid the moving ceremonies for the victims of September 11, I shuddered at the thought that this dangerous *metaphor* would soon cease to be a metaphor and become a political reality, that the feelings of solidarity with the victims would be misused to create new innocent victims and the world's feelings of solidarity with America in its suffering would quickly give way to quite different emotions. Certain metaphors need to be used with extreme caution: certain powerful expressions and evocative images can soon conjure up genies that are not easy to force back into their bottles. *No war is holy*—not even "war on terrorism"; only peace is holy. The world is already so interconnected that certain words and deeds are bound to boomerang—and that does not apply only to terrorist outrages but also to attempts to wage "war on terrorism" solely with the weapons that the terrorists deal in.

Is this situation really insoluble? The worlds of different cultures and religions have drawn closer to each other thanks to various technological inventions and economic ties, but the latter have not resulted in closer mutual understanding. Talk of "clash of civilizations" and "culture wars" hovers over us like black clouds of ominous prophecies, like *strange birds* betokening bad weather, as Kierkegaard once described himself. What can we do? There really are no quick fixes available. Long-term thinking is required, however much the blood on our own threshold understandably undermines our calm and patience. No one has a gimmick for changing the stones of hatred and violence into the bread of love, peace, and mutual understanding—and, like Jesus in the wilderness, we should have the courage to actually refuse such solutions as typical satanic temptations to abandon patience and "take a shortcut."

What is clearly most important at the present time is *to remove stones*: to weigh in our hands and hearts our sacred symbols and the words of our scriptures that could be used for "stone throwing," for instigating and justifying violence against others and hatred of difference—as indeed they have been used so frequently in the past and continue to be used.

The historical memory of nations and religious communities—and particularly in the powerful mythologies about their own past, which are frequently and dangerously revived nowadays—contains an odd mixture of memories of ancient battles, grievances suffered and the faults of others, feelings of jealousy, and unacknowledged feelings of guilt or inferiority compensated for by pride in their own predestination.

Jonathan Sacks, the Chief Rabbi of the British Commonwealth, whom I mentioned earlier, came up with a remarkable interpretation of the Bible story of Jacob's quarrel with Esau, including the well-known scene of the nocturnal wrestling bout on the banks of the Jabbok.[10] As we know, Jacob uses a ruse to obtain a blessing and a promise for which the first-born, Esau, arrives too late. In the end, however, Esau also does not leave without a blessing. Sacks comments that to be chosen does not mean that others are "not chosen." In order for us to be close to God we do not have to prevent others from having their own (possibly different) relationship with Him. (This brings to mind an even more radical statement by Levinas, another Jewish thinker: we are all chosen.)

According to Sacks, Jacob's problem was that he always wanted to be Esau, to be in Esau's place. He wrestled with him in his mother's womb, held onto him by the heel, and bought his birthright for a mess of pottage. He dressed in his clothes and when he was asked by blind Isaac, he replied: I am Esau. He did wrong and usurped a blessing. And when the hour of reckoning comes near and Esau is marching on him with a large army, Jacob is sorely afraid.

But then night comes and during it the event that changes everything. Jacob, who committed his fraud in the night of his father's blindness, is obliged to descend into the darkness of his own fear and guilt—and there do battle. He wrestles with the Unknown—and holds his own. He knows full well who his opponent is: he names the place Peniel, i.e., "It is because I have seen God face to face, and yet my life has been spared." For descending into the darkness, for not evading the battle, and for holding his own, he is given a new name: Israel—"because you have contended with divine and human beings and have prevailed."

Now Jacob-Israel no longer needs to wish to be someone else—he is himself at last. And therefore he can be reconciled with his brother. Because he has shown great strength, he can now display great humility when meeting his brother. Because he had the courage to look into the face of God in the darkness of a difficult trial, the misdeed for which he used the darkness of his father's blindness has been atoned for—and he can now look into the face of his brother in the light.

In my view, the time for *gathering stones together* is precisely that *labor in the darkness* that requires courage to descend into what is forgotten, displaced, and burdened down with guilt and debts in the "collective subconscious," and there, in the depths, tear up by the roots our mutual prejudices and animosities and heal the unhealed scars of the past. It is often also a battle, above all a battle with ourselves, and we must often suffer various wounds in the process. But we can also uncover our real identity.

Often we project onto others the things that we are unwilling or unable to acknowledge about ourselves—and this applies not only in private life, but also in relations between countries, religions, and cultures. The mechanism of projection and the emergence of pathological "enemy images" was described by Carl Gustav Jung, and in the final analysis this was the point of Jesus's challenge for us to "remove the beam from our own eye" before starting to look for "the mote" in the eyes of others. The "motes" in the eyes of others are possibly just illusions—simply shadows and projections of our own beams that we have failed to remove.

In the article mentioned earlier, Joseph Moingt wrote that what is most characteristic and valuable about Christianity is that it ushered in a *new way of being together with others.* We could say: a new culture of closeness, a new method of *making ourselves neighbors* toward others, toward those different from us. Let us not forget, though, that here too the New Testament has its roots in the Torah—let us not forget the story of Jacob and Esau.

The moment in history when so much is spoken about the danger of the "clash of civilizations" is reminiscent of that evening full of anxiety on the banks of the stream called Jabbok when the armies of the fraternal enemies were coming closer to each other. But let us not sleep through the approaching night. The night which could certainly be a difficult contest, will, if we prevail, enable us to stand the test next morning in the task of reconciliation, so that the *time of closeness* might arrive at last.

᠅

CHAPTER 10

A Time to Heal

Whenever I pass by a certain disused Prague synagogue I read on its facade the still visible but very timeworn sign: "Shalom—Peace to Those Near and Far!"

Shalom is not simply peace in the sense of absence of war and disputes between peoples and nations. It is not the peace that exudes from the eternal order of nature. Nor is it that cosmic harmony that the meditative paths of the East invite us to seek. Shalom has more to do with the history of salvation than with the natural cycles: biblical tradition is aware that that harmony was once deeply disrupted; it is aware of the hidden scar at the heart of being. It is aware of what Virgil seemingly had in mind with his mysterious verse that is difficult to translate: "sunt lacrimae rerum"—*these are the tears of things.* Shalom is *peace recovered.* It means *reconciliation* between God and people, people and nature, mutual reconciliation between people and human families, and also profound peace in the human heart—shalom is grateful thanks for healing, forgiveness, and salvation.

If, in these days, we experience shalom—as a pious Jew does, for instance, by observing and celebrating the Sabbath—we touch—

for a moment, at least—the past of the lost paradise, as well as that heavenly banquet promised in an eschatological future. It is therefore a moment not only of profound joy but also of a certain sadness and regret, emanating from our impossible longing to remain forever in that peace. At such moments we are often reluctant to leave—of course we would like "to make three tents" as the apostle Peter proposed on Mount Tabor[1]—yet at the same time we are aware that our daily pilgrimage will return us once more to the valley of everyday routine "separated from the presence of the Lord."

When the risen Jesus walks through the locked doors of fear into the midst of His disciples, He brings them His first gift—the Spirit, and He speaks in the same breath about peace and the forgiveness of sins.[2] He comes to bring them peace and give them the power to forgive sins—*He breathes on them.* That gesture recalls the act of the Creator that we read about in Genesis: "The Lord God formed man out of the clay of the ground and blew into his nostrils the breath of life, and so man became a living being."[3]

According to the Bible, man was created from the clay of the ground, from nothing, from finitude—and also from the Spirit, the principle of the God of love. When the work of the Spirit is blocked—and that blocking is called sin—he returns to nothing: "When you take away their breath, they . . . return to the dust."[4] And when God gives them back the Spirit, they are created anew;[5] they are a *new creation.* The apostles who scattered at the moment of Jesus's greatest trial "returned to their dust." Now Jesus creates them anew by breathing His Spirit into them. And with this re-*creatio* He does not simply forgive their sins, He also sends them out to pass on that forgiveness.

This act of Jesus is traditionally interpreted as the establishment of the "sacrament of reconciliation." But maybe it is something much broader: the vocation of being an "instrument of peace" (as St. Francis of Assisi prayed), of being servants of reconciliation and forgiveness.

~

Personal names in the Bible often have symbolic meaning. And like all symbols, they reveal and conceal what they symbolize at one and the same time; in this case it is a journey to the person, to the mystery of the uniqueness of every human being, the uniqueness of character and vocation. Changing the name—from Abram to Abraham, from Jacob to Israel, from Simon to Peter, from Saul to Paul—means changing the person from the very foundations; it is God's prerogative. In Revelation we are promised—if we emerge victorious from the contest of our life—a white amulet upon which will be inscribed a new name, which no one knows except the one who receives it.[6] We will discover at last our real identity. At last we will receive an answer to the question that has tormented some of us throughout our lives: Who am I really?

The tax collector's name—Zacchaeus—was probably the hellenized form of a Hebrew name denoting "pure," innocent. In the case of this particular Zacchaeus, that name must have sounded extremely ironic and given rise to malicious jokes: Mr. Pure was best known for handling dirty money. When Jesus entered his home, catharsis—cleansing, purification—occurs: repentance, conversion, healing, recovering the one who had been lost.

~

When considering how Jesus called on Zacchaeus *hidden in the leaves of the fig tree,* I can't help recalling another biblical scene: the Lord calls to Adam—after the first human couple have sinned and covered their nakedness with *fig leaves* and Adam and his wife have hidden themselves "among the trees of the garden"—and asks him "Where are you?" And Adam replies: "I heard you in the garden; but I was afraid, because I was naked, so I hid myself."[7]

Zacchaeus, who was regarded in the neighborhood as a sinner, and who subsequently admitted that he had cheated his neighbors and extorted things from them unjustly, had climbed the fig tree not only because he was short of stature. He clearly had another reason to hide and keep at a distance from the crowds. Zacchaeus realized—somewhere deep in his soul, at least—that he was a sinner, "a son of Adam." But Jesus goes on to call him in public a "son of Abraham," a son of the *father of the faith.*

Our existence too stretches between Adam and Abraham, and between the "first Adam" and the "second Adam"—Christ. Like his (and our) forefather Adam, Zacchaeus is covered by fig leaves like a sinner. Zacchaeus does not peer out of his tree with fear, however, but with eager yearning. His body is concealed, but his soul is open. And so he is able to hear and accept the invitation, which is reminiscent of the Lord's call to Abraham: Go forth!

And just as Abraham "went out, not knowing where he was to go" (Heb. 11:8), so too Zacchaeus responds to Jesus's call and decides to leave his hiding place. He comes down from his lofty observation post not knowing exactly what awaits him. Zacchaeus's descent, like Abraham's setting out on his journey, is an act of faith—faith as a readiness to obey a call and respond to an appeal. It is an act of trust and courage in entering an unsecured space. In doing so, this son of Adam already shows he is a son of Abraham, and Jesus proclaims this publicly: "... *this man too is a descendant of Abraham. For the Son of Man has come to seek and to save what was lost.*"

Jesus tells Zacchaeus what he has to do; He has come to him and showed him and the others that this man, who has been ostracized and rejected, belongs to the family of Abraham's children. Zacchaeus's repentance and recompense are not the *reason* for the salvation, which Jesus brings to his home and publicly declares in front of his neighbors. Salvation is a gift, not a reward. Jesus came and brought His gift "without prior conditions." He didn't come to impose His gift of salvation or to offer it as a commodity that Zacchaeus must first purchase through certain deeds. Nonetheless, there is always scope to accept that gift or reject it.

Zacchaeus accepts the gift initially through his trust, by *receiving the call*—he doesn't simply remain a distant, uncommitted onlooker—and then through his decision to amend his life.

The first initiative comes from the donor—Jesus. Zacchaeus was watching and searching, but he himself was already being sought. He found because he was found. The small man, who was a "big moneybags"—envied and also despised as a sinner by the same people—is now found and accepted as a son of Abraham. At that moment he no doubt grows in stature in his own eyes and in the eyes of his neighbors. Little Zacchaeus, the chief tax collector, no longer needs the pedestal of his official status, and he is now able to get rid of a large part of his wealth too, because his worth now derives from the fact that he is regarded as something precious by the Master from Nazareth, who entered his home as a guest.

Zacchaeus was once distant—and not just at the moment when he split off from the throng and escaped to his hiding place in the treetop. He was "distant" because his previous way of life placed him among the "lost," among those "who had died." Nevertheless, he was resurrected and is now close.

Because Jesus came to meet him and entered his home, Zacchaeus is now much closer to God and his neighbors because Christ is close to him. His descent from the fig tree was consummated by the fact that his confession and repentance removed the barrier of *alienation.* After all, what is sin but alienation from God, from people, from one's own self, and from one's own intrinsic purpose?

Zacchaeus finally said openly the truth about himself—insofar as he was capable of recognizing and acknowledging it at that moment. *His conscience made itself felt within him.* Nevertheless, he still speaks in the conditional: "if I have extorted anything from anyone." He clearly needs to let his conscience do its work and reveal to him exactly whom he has cheated and in what ways. Sin likes to hide itself from the sinner; the voice of conscience can easily be drowned out by the many other voices that we hear around us, or by those that originate within ourselves.

The important event has happened, however. Zacchaeus has met with Jesus and this meeting was full of joyful trust. We may therefore regard this liberating encounter as a *faith event.* Faith liberates our conscience from the bondage of lies, excuses, and forgetting—and therefore heals, revives, and brings us into the fullness of truth. In the Bible, truth is a matter of right living rather than intellectual perception; the New Testament speaks of "doing truth," "living the truth," not simply recognizing truth or speaking the truth.

Living the truth means acting responsibly, not just reacting. Reaction is behavior that is determined by what is exterior, by others, by their behavior and conduct. To act according to the "tit for tat" principle still means operating within the realm of reaction, where the action of the other determines our own. Genuinely free action comes from inside, from the shrine of conscience. However, as I have already indicated, conscience has to be awakened and liberated; it must also be nurtured and cultivated in order to mature.

Another indication of truthfulness and mature faith is the degree to which faith creates scope for conscience, the extent to which it illuminates, awakens, and reinforces conscience. A mature faith helps conscience to mature; immature faith does not trust conscience and tries to replace it with mechanical obedience to externally imposed prescriptions and proscriptions.

♂

Jesus could also have said to Zacchaeus: "Your faith has made you whole," in other words, not "you have healed yourself" (by your own powers), nor "I have healed you" (from outside and without your involvement), but "we have really encountered each other and from that encounter is born a faith that has healing and liberating effects."

What was the crucial moment of Jesus's brief encounter with Zacchaeus, i.e., what actually caused Zacchaeus's change of heart and life—his *metanoia,* his conversion? Where did the catharsis occur in this minor drama?

Let us recall another Gospel event about healing through faith. It is a story that is easy to overlook because the evangelist includes it within the narrative about a "great miracle": the raising up of the daughter of Jairus. It is the story of a woman who had suffered from hemorrhages for twelve years. She had endured much at the hands of many doctors and spent all her savings on treatment, but nothing had worked.

She had heard about Jesus and came up behind Him in the crowd and touched His cloak. She said, "If I but touch His clothes, I shall be cured." Immediately her flow of blood dried up. She felt in her body that she was healed of her affliction. Jesus, aware at once that power had gone out from Him, turned around in the crowd and asked, "Who has touched my clothes?" But His disciples said to Him, "You see how the crowd is pressing upon you, and yet you ask, 'Who touched me?' " And He looked around to see who had done it. The woman, realizing what had happened to her, approached in fear and trembling. She fell down before Jesus and told Him the whole truth. He said to her, "Daughter, your faith has saved you. Go in peace and be cured of your affliction."[8]

Here again it is the story of a person called by Jesus from the shelter of her anonymity who, later, before Jesus and the gaze of the others, tells her entire unconcealed truth. One contemporary theologian offers an in-depth psychological interpretation of the story.[9] Chronic hemorrhaging is one of the psychosomatic disorders or illnesses that manifest "the body's language," what a particular person has pushed into her unconscious and doesn't want to speak or know anything about. The woman is wounded in the very shrine of her womanhood and most likely bears within her some serious trauma in an intimate area, her sexuality. Her hemorrhaging of many years not only is physically debilitating, painful, and embarrassing, but it also deprives her of the right to any sort of closeness, excluding her from human and religious fellowship. According to the Jewish canons, a hemorrhaging woman was ritually unclean and was not allowed to attend worship in the synagogue; she was also not allowed to touch anyone, and no one was allowed to touch her. Her compulsive longing for human closeness, for human touch, drives her to an action that breaks through her prescribed isolation: she touches Jesus. She touches Him surreptitiously from behind, from within the throng. Jesus does not want her to seize her healing in this manner, however. He seeks her face—and in a way He "calls her by name," thus destroying her anonymity. The disciples think it is a silly question: *the whole crowd* is pressing against Him, so how can He identify the touch of a single person? But for Jesus, no one is drowned and no one is lost in the *whole crowd*. For Him, no person and no touch is anonymous, impersonal, or interchangeable. The woman approaches, and after years of hiding and isolation she "tells the whole truth" in front of everyone. And at that moment of truth she is freed from her malady.

Her faith—which, in Jesus's words, has saved her—already manifested itself, however, in her touch, that crazy gesture that was full of yearning and trust. It was an act in contravention of the Law—after all, her touch rendered Jesus ritually unclean. It was a sin according to strict interpretations of the Law. And yet Jesus understood what she was saying by her action, and He interpreted it as an act of salvation. What she started to say in her body language—which had hitherto manifested itself only in blood and pain—she finished in words, when she fell down before Jesus and "told Him the whole truth."

That woman's faith—like that of Zacchaeus—is not "rational endorsement of the truths of faith"; it has nothing to do with rational conviction and cannot be expressed in dogmatic formulas. It springs from longing, and part of it is trust. It happens as part of an unexpected, unplanned, and (at the conscious level, at least) unwanted "face-to-face encounter"—and culminates in the courage to face the truth.

Those people could feel Jesus's *power*. They felt that He was someone who spoke and acted "as one having authority, and not as their scribes."[10] They are bound to have recognized also that it was a power of a different order than the kind wielded by the mighty of this world, one that is associated with violence and oppression. Zacchaeus, the woman healed of her hemorrhage, and many others that Jesus encounters, are neither able nor feel the need to express their experience with Jesus in the form of a confession such as that made by Peter at Caesarea Philippi,[11] and certainly not in the theological and dogmatic language used by the church in later centuries.

When, in their encounters with Jesus, as we read in the Gospels, people glimpsed and experienced the lightning of God's power and God's magnificent fullness, they tended to express it through gestures (such as by falling on their faces, kneeling, or bowing) and cries of joy ("Raboni!" "My Lord and my God!"), not in the form of polished theological terms and theories. The confession of faith of the hemorrhaging woman was her furtive touch (which was, as we mentioned, problematical in religious terms as it was ritually impure). Zacchaeus's gesture is his descent from the treetop, and his confession of faith is his resolve to rebuild his life—and his property relations—in the spirit of justice and atonement. His reception of Jesus is not a matter of profound speculations about the essence of Jesus or agreement with teaching about Jesus or Jesus's own teaching, but simply of opening the door of his home—an opening preceded by Jesus's surprising request to spend time in his company.

Scripture doesn't tell us whether Zacchaeus or the woman cured of her bleeding regarded Jesus as the promised Messiah of the Jews, and it is unlikely that they would have understood the expressions "God's only begotten son" or "God-Man." Nevertheless, by trusting in that man they also experienced in their own way that "whoever has seen me has seen the Father,"[12] that Jesus's words and deeds, His entire humanity, are "a window through which human beings can see God at work."

While it is true that our theological notions and the theories we advance in our efforts to express the mystery of Jesus draw on the philosophical terminology of subsequent centuries, there is a sense in which they are rooted most deeply in these Gospel stories and the events revealed to us by them. Teaching about the divinity of Jesus did not emerge initially in the minds of theologians; it was preceded by the apostle Thomas's joyous cry of "My Lord and my God" when he touched the wounds of the risen Christ. It was definitely not Thomas's intention to pass metaphysical judgment on the nature of Jesus; he simply allowed his joy to gush forth, and he spontaneously reached for the expressions in his own vocabulary that struck him as most apt, at that moment, to express such immense joy.

Maybe we should try sometimes to renew our religious language by plunging those expressions we often overemploy and our dust-covered definitions into that original fount of faith, into the liberating and life-transforming joy that was experienced during their encounters with Jesus by people such as the apostle Thomas, the apostle to the apostles, Mary Magdalene, Zacchaeus, or the woman cured of hemorrhage. Maybe then we would find it easier to encourage the Zacchaeuses of our day to come out of their hiding places and change their lives. Maybe then we could better understand the quiet language of furtive touches and prove capable of creating a space for trust, in which people can speak their whole truth and so be cured of their afflictions.

ꝫ

When I was telling the story of Zacchaeus to the members of the Czech parliament, it also occurred to me that the church in our country owes society something else, apart from "addressing Zacchaeus." I feel that we have failed in something that is one of the basic tasks of Christians—and which is also, after all, related to the story of Zacchaeus—*being experts in the field of forgiveness and reconciliation.*

There was a time when I thought that one of the hardest moral challenges—but also one of the greatest opportunities to be morally adult—is to retain one's integrity at a time of persecution, during a period when freedom is denied. I subsequently realized that it is even harder to do so on the threshold of newly restored freedom. After the fall of a totalitarian regime or after the end of a civil war, heroes and victims of the previous era remain mingled in one society with the culprits and collaborators, as well as with those who managed to "survive" at the cost of various compromises, both acknowledged and unacknowledged. When the ruins and barricades are being cleared away—including those that remained within people themselves—the entire society is dirtied for a while by all the dust that is kicked up in the process. Following a battle, neither the victors nor the vanquished tend to be clean; there is a need for overall and thorough cleansing. But beware of those who seek to undertake such a demanding task too soon and too vehemently!

It is not always easy to distinguish between those who were mainstays of the dictatorship, those who acted according to their sincere—albeit from our standpoint entirely false—convictions, and those who were just cynically self-seeking, between those who seduced others and those who were naively seduced. How does one tell apart those who gradually turned away from the regime because they recognized their error and their conscience was awakened, and those who, in the end, switched to the opposition simply because they had been cast aside as being no longer of use to those in power. Moreover, documents can turn up many years later that reveal the failings of some of those who were regarded as "decent" and "unblemished," even among those who were considered active opponents of the regime, and it has often turned out that they had carefully concealed their behavior not only from others but even from their own consciences. And very often, after the fall of a dictatorship, one finds that the most radical judges and avengers include those who themselves failed shamefully and now try to justify themselves to themselves and others, and to furnish themselves with an alibi *post facto*.

In our country, the transition from dictatorship to democracy occurred without any phase of revolutionary settling of accounts. There has been no "Jacobin period," nothing akin to the Nuremburg trials. No one has come to the slightest harm, not a drop of blood has been spilt. The world spoke appreciatively about the "Velvet Revolution" that took place like a short-lived street festival. It is undoubtedly a good thing that no "spirit of vengeance" was awakened nor any "witch hunt" unleashed. But was it really a matter of forgiveness and reconciliation? Wasn't it the other extreme (the opposite of murderous settling of accounts) that happened, i.e., the *disparagement of blame*? The slogan "let us draw a line under the past" was no doubt well intentioned: let us not take vengeance, let us not return evil for evil, "let us not be like them." But it was actually interpreted and implemented as: let us forget as fast and completely as we possibly can!

Something similar occurred in almost all the post-Communist countries. Because we spared ourselves the painful process of reconciliation and healing in our society, that society was morally debilitated. Wounds were not healed but simply covered up—and they started to fester; the poison gradually began to spread through the entire organism. The haze that allowed the illusion of apparent unity to be created and in which the difference between dissident and informer was quickly erased, did not pay off: the haze thickened and the light of truth started to fade.

In that haze the former political elite quietly slipped out of the world of political and police power into the field of economic power and, thanks to their accumulated capital of money, contacts, and information, they once again started to dominate society.

No doubt the conviction that "no one was either completely white or completely black" was essentially correct. However, instead of encouraging understanding among people, it just created more thick gray fog, in which the barrier between truth and lies was increasingly eroded. The fear of oversimple judgments led to a loss of sound judgment and an ominous relativization of all moral values. It is definitely a good thing that the domination of one ideology did not give way to the domination of a different ideology, equally intolerant and blinkered. However, the principle of "every-thing goes" opened the gates to forces that slowly started to turn freedom into chaos and furnish the enemies of democracy and open society with additional arguments. Those who called attention to this development and the risks it entailed were despised and ridiculed by many as naively idealistic moralists and suspected of wanting to threaten and restrict freedom—particularly by those who really were threatening and misusing freedom.

Many believed (and they still do), that Czech society would al-ways contain a certain residue of democratic culture that would pre-vent that development from going as far, on the threshold of the new millennium, as it had in the surrounding countries, particularly Rus-sia and several former Soviet republics. But wasn't that democratic culture already lost a long time ago, just after World War II, when a dreadfully destructive wave of development gradually reached us from Russia, development almost everyone in those days thought would assume a different form here, and take place in a more mod-erate and civilized manner, when it was believed that Communism with a more democratic and humane face would assert itself in our country? In a certain respect—and particularly in its relations with the churches and religion—Communism behaved in our country even less humanely than in any of the neighboring countries.

Others point out that scandals and corruption are an attendant feature of democracy, and not only at its halting early stages, that they are a burning issue, particularly nowadays, even in the "old and mature democracies"—in other words, what we now confront in the post-Communist countries should not perturb us too much. It may be assumed that many of the negative phenomena occurred not only behind the impenetrable walls of totalitarian regimes, but also in the open space of free societies—and the fact that we are confronted with them more often and visibly is chiefly because these things are more publicized these days in the mass media.

Moreover, we are gradually becoming more and more involved in global society, in which classical democracy is logically finding itself in crisis. We are capable of handling democratic mechanisms within the framework of nation-states but, whether we like it or not, their role is clearly weakening. Supranational corporations—operating in areas that the mechanisms of classical democracy cannot reach—will continue to wield decisive power in the economic and political spheres. Citizens, particularly of smaller countries, are increasingly aware of the dwindling power of the representatives they elect, and therefore, particularly among the younger generation, fewer and fewer are ready or willing to take part in elections at all and be involved, at least in this way, in political life. Politics is becoming part of "show business," and more and more citizens follow it with detachment, boredom, and distaste through the mirror of the media, or simply joke about it and make ironic or indignant comments as they do during sports programs on TV, but they have no sense of being fellow players. They have no sense of being drawn into the game, no sense of shared responsibility. They have no sense of being "called by name." But whereas dictatorships and totalitarian regimes largely thrive on the political passivity of the majority of citizens, the survival of democracy depends on the proportion of "freeloaders" unwilling to invest their energy in civic life not exceeding a certain tolerable percentage.

The victory of dictatorships over democratic regimes—always only temporary, so far, thank God—always started when the specific form of democracy lost its credibility in the eyes of a large number of citizens. The credibility of the young democracies in the post-Communist world depends also on how they manage to "come to terms with the past," with the moral legacy of the totalitarian regimes, how they manage to unite a divided society without incurring a bloody settling of accounts or a cynical disparagement of blame.

I recall conversations with the American ambassador to Prague about the ending of apartheid in South Africa and how the "reconciliation rituals" that had occurred there were rooted in the ethos of the Christian faith. He asked me why something similar was not taking place in the post-Communist world.[13] Those conversations took place a number of years ago, before the unfortunate war in Iraq. I expect I would ask him nowadays whether that war, however it turns out, has not left society seriously divided, not only in Iraq, but also in the United States. Won't America also have to undergo an enormous catharsis, even more profound than after the Vietnam War or the Watergate affair? Won't the need for the reconciliation and healing that we are now talking about in relation to the post-Communist world be also an issue for the American nation before long?

Yes, we Christians ought to rise to the occasion as "experts in reconciliation" and show in practical ways—starting with things happening in the ranks of our own churches—that forgiveness and reconciliation are something quite different from shortsighted and careless "forgetting" or "turning one's coat." It is a long-term process of rebirth that can be as demanding, arduous, and painful as birth itself. It comprises acknowledging and confessing faults and a process of penance—and at the end of it former culprits can emerge much profounder and more authentic human beings than those who once simply went with the tide and never "got their hands dirty" or "lost face." Also relevant here is what the Gospel has to say about how, when a woman is in labor, she is in anguish because her hour has arrived, but when she has given birth to a child, she no longer remembers the pain because of her joy that a child has been born into the world. I expect that moment of pain cannot be hurdled too quickly or carelessly forgotten—otherwise the hopes for a new life and a new beginning could miscarry.

We believe that God's forgiveness is a gift of grace, given freely and without the presupposition of merit, and that all it needs is to expose our hearts to Him. However, forgiveness and reconciliation as an interpersonal and social process is an arduous activity. As Christians, to forgive is one of our fundamental moral duties—but I hasten to add that in certain circumstances it can be a very hard task. "Healing memory"—a favorite expression of Pope John Paul II in connection with the church's penance before entering the new millennium—assumes a readiness not to simply shift the many traumas and painful memories of wrongs suffered into the subconscious. It applies both to the memory of individuals and to "collective memory," which is essential for the culture of society, for forming and preserving its identity.

Wherever dramatic social changes have not given rise to public debate about the past, including its painful, dark, and guilt-burdened aspects, where there has been no verbalization of the unsaid that could lead to catharsis and reconciliation, "division of memory" remains. Therefore a profound division of society remains also, however much it is disguised by "oblivion" and "feigned forgiveness." The nation—like the church—is a "community of memory." The past needs to be reflected on and transformed—such as through art, public debate, historical research, preserving "places of memory," etc.—to allow it to become part of the collective memory. So long as society fails to relate to its past in this way, fragmentation of memory occurs. After all, each group experienced the past in a different way and from a different standpoint, so that it remembers it differently, and if social dialogue does not take place, this permanent fragmentation of memory prevents the real healing and mending of society.

There are certain misdeeds of the past, unhealed wounds of yesteryear (and the crimes of the totalitarian regimes are certainly among them) that are impossible to remedy and atone for in a simple way, ones that are hard to "forget"—and in a certain sense they must not be forgotten—and they cannot be expunged even by the usual mechanisms of law, courts, and penalties. There are wrongs that "cry out to heaven." And in these specific situations, where human instruments of law and the social therapy of public debate have been exhausted, an indispensable act of a spiritual nature is appropriate, namely, forgiveness. It is not by any means a question of careless forgetting, but of consciously waiving judgment and consigning the entire matter to the competency of that seat of justice and mercy that "this world" does not have at its disposition.

The theologian Johann Baptist Metz recalls that whereas the surrounding nations had their consolatory mythologies that explained in various ways the horrors of history, biblical Israel remained a "landscape of outcry." The psalms and the prophets offer no soothing rationalizations of what has happened, but instead they submit the cry of a suffering people to the one *who is to come*. What no human power or justice is capable of remedying or healing must be left open for God until the hour of eschatological judgment.

The story of Zacchaeus is a story of conversion, forgiveness, penance, and being received once more. It is a story of reconciliation and salvation: "For the Son of Man has come to seek and to save what was lost."

In Luke's account of Zacchaeus's conversion there is no mention of contrition in the sense of "feelings of penitence" that so many homilies and pious writings have tried so fervently to foster. Zacchaeus does not agonize: when he talks about giving half of his property to the poor and compensating those he cheated fourfold, it is due to the euphoria he feels at the presence of Jesus in his home. He acts more like the man in Jesus's parable who found a treasure hidden in a field and in his elation sold everything in order to buy the field and thus acquire his rare find.

The Indian Jesuit Anthony de Mello has pointed out that nowhere in the Gospels does Jesus ask sinners to express regret— He has no place for regret in the process of conversion. This process is a thoroughly joyous event. Distress about sin has always already been mixed with joy and gratitude at the gift of forgiveness and generous acceptance. People can only realize their sinfulness if they are already standing outside the dark cell of sin; they can see sin only in the light of mercy. Usually sinners do not see their sin, or they do not see it truthfully; they are ensnared by the darkness. To see one's sins with real clarity is the privilege of saints. They often truly wept over their sins, but at the same time they knew how to praise God for His mercy.

If I see my sin, I ought not to let the sight of it bewitch or dismay me, but instead I should turn toward the source of the light that allowed me to see it and acknowledge it. If we look backward all the time, we could end up like Lot's wife and become "pillars of salt" rather than the *salt of the earth*. Yes, there are moments when one looks at one's failures and discovers that at this particular moment one has nothing to offer God but a broken heart, as is sung in David's well-known psalm of repentance. However, in that story about David's sin and repentance, which the psalm in question is usually associated with, we read that at the very moment when his servants were expecting David to sink into the deepest depression, he stopped weeping and fasting, washed his face, and sat down to eat in order to strengthen himself for his new life.

De Mello believes that instead of stressing regret as the major component of the process of repentance and conversion, our catechisms should emphasize trust in the power of God's forgiveness and a willingness to forgive our own enemies. The failure to trust in God's power to do something substantial with the world and with myself is regarded by that Indian Jesuit as the only really tragic sin— "a sin against the Holy Spirit."

ぷ

An indispensable step on the path to forgiveness and reconciliation is a firm determination not to allow oneself to be drawn into the spiral of vengeance that escalates the injuries suffered. It is not even enough to want to halt the spirit of vengeance that never stops calling for evil to be multiplied, at the boundary of simple justice: "tit for tat," "an eye for an eye and a tooth for a tooth" (and nothing else). For even in this case it is behavior that is determined by the other, a criterion that is forced on us from outside.

That is why Jesus countered the principle of "tit for tat" with the rule "as God does to me, so I'll do to you"—and He demonstrates that we all live from the gift of God's generous forgiveness, from God's patience. And if I have God's patience with me, why should I not tolerate my neighbor's weakness? Why should I try to play the role of an all-knowing judge? Should I not instead offer corrective experience to someone in the clutches of evil and show him an entirely different kind of reaction, an entirely different quality of behavior?

But Jesus is not naive, and He does not steer us toward the naive conviction that generous love will always pay off. Such behavior must be prepared for sacrifice, for defeat—and at the very least we will be regarded as naive fools, just as He was—and it therefore assumes great moral strength and freedom from our selfish calculations. Nevertheless, only courage like this is capable of leading the world out of the satanically initiated spiral of hatred and violence.

"S'ist schwer zu sein a Jid"—it's hard to be a Jew—is what one of my dearest Jewish friends says on various occasions, with the typically rueful smile of his people. It's not particularly easy to be a Christian either, if we read the Gospel attentively and take it seriously. Only through the power of great love and persevering faith can this cross become "a yoke that is easy."[14] But we must not turn traitor or desert in the continuing battle with evil in which our life stories are rooted. Only if we refuse to let evil manipulate us into adopting its methods and its style of battle can we receive at the end the *white amulet* on which we will read at last who we really are.

✣

CHAPTER 11

St. Zacchaeus

As my reflections near their conclusion, I would like to suggest another version of the apocrypha about Zacchaeus:

Zacchaeus fulfilled everything he had solemnly promised to Jesus—and did many other good things besides. He died at a ripe old age, surrounded by his loving family and his grateful countrymen from Jericho and miles around. In him the promise was fulfilled that this son of Abraham would receive salvation. He rests in the bosom of Abraham—even though because of various major bureaucratic obstacles (such as the fact that he was not baptized) he cannot be declared a saint by the relevant Vatican congregation; Jesus not only did not begrudge him a halo, He entrusted him with a quite specific mission in the communication between heaven and earth: St. Zacchaeus became the patron and protector of the eternal seekers, the "peepers-out." And, surprisingly, his role is not to *convert* them (any old saint could do that), but to watch over their patience in the anteroom of faith. After all, God has to have His people even outside the doors of church buildings; He has them also in the intricate labyrinths of searching, which the "pious" have never got lost in or even ventured into—and it is there that God's children also need someone to protect them and intercede for them. Even on the "other bank" there are many of those to whom Jesus's words "you are not far from the Kingdom of God" also apply.

Who is to transmit those words to them if not ourselves? But how are we to do it so that the tidings are really a joyful message? How is Jesus's news to be addressed to them *by name,* so that what they hear from our lips does not scare them off? How can we ensure that it is perceived truly as a friendly invitation that appeals to their freedom and not as an obtrusive attempt to proselytize them, an arrogant appropriation of those who don't want to belong to us? How are we to show not just tact and "pastoral foresight" but also the love that—in Levinas's words—allows others to be other, respects their otherness, and does not seek to erase all differences and convert others to our side straightaway?

When the Catholic writer François Mauriac read one particular text by the philosopher Gabriel Marcel, he wrote to him asking: "Child, why were you not one of us long ago?" Marcel discerned therein a call from God, and he converted and was baptized. Can it be that easy, and is that the right way? I also occasionally find myself saying as I observe certain people: Child, why were you not one of us long ago? I often say it not only in respect of those I see standing timidly in the church porch, as I once did, but also in the case of many people who have started to reflect seriously and honestly about important issues, or who experience to the full some genuine happiness or grief.

I know these things from reading that inspired book by C. S. Lewis, *The Screwtape Letters,* which I give to every new convert as compulsory reading. In it, the young, inexperienced demon, who has been given the task of tempting a young intellectual Christian convert, boasts of his successes—but he is always immediately rebuked by his experienced uncle, a senior member of the satanic hierarchy. When the young demon whoops over the fact that his charge has been reflecting on a book by some atheist philosopher, the old demon is appalled: Don't let him! Anyone who really reasons is already on the Enemy's (God's) home ground! Our domain is the realm of simple slogans, such as "That's not scientific! That's old-fashioned" and so on. (That fear about the study of atheist philosophers brings to mind what Father Tischner used to say about never yet having come across someone who had abandoned the faith because of reading Marx's *Capital*, whereas he knew a lot of people who had lapsed as the result of their priest's stupid preaching.) The senior demon also felt it was dangerous when people experienced genuine grief or real joy, or even the simple enjoyment of a quiet autumn walk past an old mill, because it could bring them closer to the Enemy "up there." "Down there" they rejoice when, instead of real sadness or real happiness, people cultivate dejection, world-weariness, and self-pity in their souls, what Czechs call "a rotten mood"—once highlighted in a particular speech by Václav Havel. This is a perfect seedbed in which the demons can truly revel and where their whispering can take root and spread "like mushrooms after rain," as we also say in our country.

How, when, and whether at all are we to tell those "far off" that they are actually close to us, without alienating them? May the prayers of St. Zacchaeus bring us wisdom!

✢

In her prayers—which were unknown to anyone but God, and which we learned about only from her diary many years later, and after the veil of censorship had been lifted from it along with the sickly sugarcoating of her pious publishers—Thérèse de Lisieux accepted those distant ones silently into her pain, into her solidarity, and at the same table. She experienced "the thoughts of the worst materialists" and prayed for her atheist brothers without their knowing a thing about it—is that good or bad?

It is conceivable that her idea of atheists still being in darkness—albeit unaware of the fact because, unlike her, they had not yet experienced God's closeness—could have exasperated and alienated even more those atheists who regarded themselves as enlightened. When reading those touching words of the dying nun, it often struck me as an afterthought (because I'm almost constantly assailed by the "arguments of the worst skeptics") that even those words could be interpreted as an expression of that unfortunate urge of many Christians, who, as Dietrich Bonhoeffer sarcastically put it, try to persuade a happy person that they are actually unhappy, and bring people to their knees with two blows: "You're sinful!" and "You are going to die!"—before pulling out their kindly recipe for salvation. Bonhoeffer appeals to Christians to give up their voyeuristic prying into human sins and weaknesses and instead to talk to people in good faith when they are strong, not just when they are weak, and when they are happy, not just when they are in tears.

Sometimes it is necessary, of course, to help people remove the rosy spectacles of optimism, turn off the distorting artificial light, and take a look at the unpleasant truths too—and make use of that art of faith to *reinterpret,* to show things from the other side. It was an art mastered by the prophets of Israel—and it could make them very unpopular—when at moments of weeping they would bring consolation, while at moments of false peace they were capable of shouting at the world that this was not peace. (In this respect, powerful, prophetic faith can perform a similar service to that of powerful, prophetic art, particularly literature, painting, or creative film.)

Nietzsche was an accomplished demystifier, a passionate demasker of illusions, a master at showing things from the other side and revealing the opposite of what many things seemed to be and what they purported to be. He was capable of uncovering "nihilism" as the hidden basis of the entire metaphysical tradition of the West, or the resentment and "spirit of revenge" behind the Christian ethic of compassion. Did he know himself, at least in some corner of his soul—or did anyone try to tell him—that his rejection of compassion possibly concealed a passionate "genius of compassion"? Or didn't he himself hint at that slightly in his statement that Zarathustra was "the most pious of all those who believe not in God"?

Thérèse de Lisieux underwent her Good Friday, when her vomiting of blood revealed the truth of her illness and ushered in her final year of inner darkness and trials, just a few months after Nietzsche's Good Friday, that moment in Turin when the philosopher rushed to protect a horse from the carter's whip, an event that triggered his insanity. They were both to know their "Holy Saturday," the time of God's greatest hiddenness, the day in the shadow of the cross when the Resurrection, albeit close, seems to be out of sight, hidden by mere illusions and unfulfilled expectations. It was a time when the deranged Nietzsche signed himself "The Crucified" or "Dionysus," and when Thérèse endured her "night of nothingness," when she "ate the bread of tears" and she was assailed by the "arguments of the worst materialists."

What did Nietzsche's madness consist of, and what was the

meaning of the event that opened the door to it? Was Nietzsche's derangement simply the mental "superstructure" of an organic illness, or was his madness merely feigned or simulated, as some surmised? Was it divine punishment for his blasphemy, as certain Christians liked to believe? Or was it perhaps a strange kind of that *mania*, that divine possession, that Plato mentions as one of the paths to understanding and feeling the most fundamental things?

In his excellent study on Nietzsche and Dostoyevsky,[1] Richard E. Friedman first highlights the striking resemblance between what happened in Turin and the dream that Raskolnikov has during the night before the murder (and which would seem to reflect some traumatic memory from Dostoyevsky's childhood), about a small boy trying in vain to prevent a drunken carter beating to death his exhausted horse. Friedman then proceeds to use Freud's study on "the case of the young Hans" (a boy suffering with a phobia about horses) and the play *Equus* by Peter Shaffer (about a boy who creates his own religion—horse worship—after his atheist father tears a crucifix down from the wall) in order to demonstrate, via a masterful analysis, that in the imagination of boys the horse often symbolizes the father, and how people's experience with their own fathers affects their notion of God.

I have frequently pondered on that fateful flash of sympathy that finally thrust Nietzsche—who so often teetered on the edge of nonextinct volcanoes—into the maw of the volcano of madness. After all, sympathy was precisely the emotion for which Nietzsche berated Christianity! Did he himself not write on God's death certificate in *Zarathustra* the diagnosis: "of his pity for man hath God died"?

But maybe Nietzsche himself in his heart of hearts—to the very brim of his conscious mind—was abounding with compassion (maybe he was a *genius of compassion*) until one day that suppressed compassion exploded and inundated his conscious mind with the scorching lava and dust from that explosion. Can we detect beneath all that the Pompeii of his compassion? "Of his pity for man hath God died"; did not Nietzsche go mad from his excessive compassion, an all-embracing, boundless compassion that he did not acknowledge even to himself, maybe even a compassion for a God that people (including His worshippers) had forgotten?

Nietzsche's Turin experience is similar to conversion, to those lightning conversions like Augustine's. But in Nietzsche's case everything must always be contrariwise: instead of enlightenment, obscurity, instead of light, darkness. Or maybe he had rejected so many times already the call of "tole, lege"—take and read, which Augustine had once deciphered from a child's song in a garden, that this *anticonversion* had to take place? Perhaps there was no real Christian around to show him earlier that his frantic attacks on faith and compassion were a way of resisting the compassion and faith that he carried deep inside himself, no one to dare to ask him previously, "Child, why aren't you one of us by now?" or tell him, "You are not far from the Kingdom of God!" Was there really not one Christian ready to show him that they sat at the same table and ate together "the bread of tears"?

Or was Nietzsche's madness just playacting? Could it have been a prophetic performance that was intended to convince the world of his day of its madness—just as when the Old Testament prophets acted out their seemingly absurd pantomimes, through which God sent His messages—Ezekiel's digging a hole in the wall and setting out with the exile's bundle over his shoulder,[2] his bizarre cooking,[3] or his business with wooden sticks?[4] Maybe it wasn't enough for Nietzsche to send the world the message of God's death via his *madman* in the *The Gay Science*? Maybe *he had to become a madman himself,* to cry to the world not just through his writings but also through his fate: What has become of God? How come his absence leaves you cold and indifferent? Who will assume the responsibility for what we have done? What is to follow now? What is the time now ripe for?

In his entire life and work Nietzsche was a Don Quixote, the knight of the mournful countenance. While we may not agree with the answers he obtained in the course of his campaign, which ended so strangely, at least we must not ignore the questions that drove him to seek them. When people fail to find the right answers, the questions they leave behind must be all the more of an adventuresome challenge to us! When I hear about how quickly many Christians dismiss Nietzsche, and how they all too quickly explain his radical critique of Christianity as being a result of his madness, and sometimes explain his madness as being a divine punishment, I say to myself: *It's Sancho Panza talking through them*—Sancho, who *without Quixote* is a narrow-minded oaf.

چ

The message about the death of God—as we indicated earlier—was placed in the mouth of a *madman*; after all, fools were the only ones permitted to speak the truth, even at the courts of royalty. Shortly before her death, the philosopher Simone Weil, a great seeker after God—and whose death was attributed by the coroner to her actions while the "balance of her mind" was disturbed—included in a letter to her parents a most splendid reflection on the role of fools as messengers of truth in Shakespeare's plays and about the mournful, wise eyes of the fool/dwarf Sebastian de Morra in Velázquez's celebrated painting in the Prado: "In this world, only those people who have fallen to the lowest degree of humiliation, far below beggary, who are not just without any social consideration but are regarded by all as being deprived of that foremost human dignity, reason itself—only those people, in fact, are capable of telling the truth. All the others lie. The worst tragedy of the madman is that no one listens to him, no one takes him seriously, nobody recognizes that he is speaking the truth. To know the truth at the price of profound degradation, to be able to speak it and not be heard by anyone—is that the mystery of these mournful eyes?"[5]

"Mental imbalance," that was how the doctor at Middlesex Hospital in August 1943—amid the madness of war—explained why the sick Simone Weil refused to eat. But isn't there something symbolic in the deaths of Thérèse de Lisieux, Nietzsche, and Simone Weil, regardless of what the doctors' diagnoses say? Hunger—a hunger for God, and literally a hunger for sacraments, baptism, and the Eucharist, was a theme that pervaded the later writings of Simone Weil. Although she herself wrote sublime passages about the sacraments, she refused baptism until the very last moment. She consciously wished to remain in the "anteroom of the church," saying she was more ready to die for the church than to join it. She denied herself what she yearned for. She was convinced that the hunger of yearning can bring one closer to grace in the same way as the sacraments. In a profound reflection on the mystery of Easter, she remains in the silence of Holy Saturday. She writes that the cross itself is enough for her.

Her close friends interpreted her life and the mystery of her death differently than the doctor who treated her. Richard Rees wrote that her refusal to eat was a suicidal act in the sense that one might describe as suicidal activity someone's refusal to get into a lifeboat, so as to leave space for others. To the finding of "unbalanced mind" he appends the question whether Simone Weil did not in fact spend her whole life striving to reestablish the balance, to counterbalance those whose minds were *too* "well balanced," and in reality were indifferent and self-centered.

Maybe her *foolishness*—her refusal to accept physical or spiritual food, her remaining on the threshold, permanently "waiting on God" (which is also the title of her best-known book)—was also some kind of prophetic message, a mirror placed before our world—in the very midst of that long and insane night of slaughter, "far from all suns."

జ

One of the fathers of the psychology of religion, the American philosopher William James, distinguished between two human types: "sick souls" and "healthy-minded people," and he indicated that each of those human types has a different path to God— "healthy-minded" via gratitude for the harmony of the world, the others generally through a crisis that provides them with an opportunity for "rebirth." The three figures we have reencountered once more in this chapter would undoubtedly be classified by James among the "sick souls," of which he himself was one, but probably not just because he considered them more interesting and deeper than people of the other, "problem-free" variety.

None of the three, however, during their *nighttime* on the brink of death, shows evidence of any particular type of conversion or "rebirth." As far as we can judge, Thérèse persevered in her passionate love for God, which survived even the eclipse of her faith. Nietzsche continued to wrestle passionately with God. And Simone remained passionately and hungrily waiting.

Did all those three paths meet in the end? Did they eventually intersect—even though they may appear from our perspective parallel and nonparallel—at the *Omega Point,* which aroused such passion in the lives of each of them, albeit in different ways? Only in the case of Thérèse are we assured by the church (by its continued reverence and its act of canonization) that her path really ended in God's embrace; the church is unable to tell us anything about the other two. But God has His own favorites, whose names are jealously guarded *in pectore,* in the intimacy of His heart, and He doesn't even divulge them to the Vatican Congregation for the Causes of Saints.

Let us commend the eternal fate not only of those two but of many other (in some ways) similar human beings—as well as the fate of their messages, searchings, struggles, expectations, and questions—to the intercession of St. Zacchaeus.

CHAPTER 12

ﾞﾉﾗ

Eternal Zacchaeus

Perhaps the foregoing apocrypha about Zacchaeus and his subsequent life was too simply optimistic to end a book that in so many ways argues against simplistic answers to tricky spiritual questions. A different, more complicated one is called for.

Let us assume that it did not take so long for our friend Zacchaeus to start forgetting about his meeting with Jesus, but that he actually forgot it fairly rapidly, and well and truly, even before he had managed to seek out all those he had cheated and recompense them as he had promised. It soon occurred to him that what he had declared before Jesus and his neighbors was too radical—he'd simply been a bit hasty at that moment: such things can happen, can't they?! And so, bit by bit, Zacchaeus returned to his old way of life.

It was only in his declining years, on one of the days of repentance between Rosh Hashanah, the New Year celebration, and Yom Kippur, the Day of Atonement, that he recalled all his erstwhile intentions and resolutions, but it had been such a long time ago that it was almost too late for him to make up for what he had neglected. So he fell on his face before the Lord and asked Him to impose a suitable penance on him.

God is merciful—and besides, Zacchaeus is a son of Abraham. So He imposed on him a penitential task—one that would take many centuries. Like Ahasuerus, he would be obliged to wander the world, traveling from town to town, from one refuge to another, and when he arrived at somewhere new he must listen attentively from a particular distance to everything that went on around him and to what people said. His release would come *the moment that he recognized for sure Christ's voice among the rest.*

Poor old Zacchaeus—the things he had to listen to in the course of those centuries! All the false prophets that he came across, some of them even invoking Jesus's name, some of them speaking so convincingly that the little fellow would be on the very brink of leaning out of his new fig tree—but always something would stay the hand that was eagerly reaching out for a branch to climb down, and something inside him would say: That's not Him yet! That's not yet Christ's rich and pure voice as I heard it that time in Jericho! You'll have to go on waiting! And so he obeyed and waited and waited, and went on listening over and over again.

What might he be listening to in our days?

༈

There is a college in Rome where I lived for a while. Among the community of seminarists and priests was a very old priest who was almost deaf and blind. He would spend most of his time in the chapel in silent self-absorption—it was either profound meditation or light sleep; no one was ever sure. From time to time—most often at an entirely unexpected moment—he would break his silence with some utterance, which could elicit debate about whether it was an ambiguous oracle of the prophetic spirit or an unambiguous sign of senility. During one service in the chapel when the Gospel reading ended with Jesus's question "But when the Son of Man comes, will he find faith on earth?" there came from the back, from deep within the old priest's meditative monologue, the loud answer: "Hardly, hardly!"

On that occasion, amid the scarcely suppressed salvos of laughter from the seminarists present, a number of dismal questions came to my mind: What if, at the end of the ages, Jesus found on earth *a church* but no *faith*? What if he found *religion*—even in its present, widely commented, globally flourishing form—but not what he was seeking—*faith*? What if he found a hundred attractive schools of *spirituality,* but not what really matters to him—*faith*?

Maybe the wanderings of the penitent Zacchaeus now take him to the premises of churches, religions, and spiritual movements, and still in none of them can he hear the voice of Christ, the pure voice that he now recalls so well. . . .

᠎᠎ᠵ᠊

Will Christ find faith on earth? A "small" faith, at least?

In one of my previous books I pleaded for "small faith" against "great faith."[1] That is how I provocatively interpret (to the rightful horror of many exegetes) Jesus's answer to the disciples' request for Him to "increase their faith," when He speaks about faith the size of a mustard seed.[2] In that book I asked: Is not Jesus telling them and us—and us in particular—that our faith is "too great" and that it will be capable of remarkable things *only if it becomes as small as a mustard seed*?

Isn't our faith *too big* (and too heavy and unwieldy) in the sense that it is burdened with too many of our notions and ideas, that it is *too human?* Maybe it will only be truly a living faith when it becomes *the faith of God*—because what is of God always appears small, weak, and foolish in this world. For did not God make foolish what is great, strong, and firm in the eyes of the world?[3]

Maybe the faith that God prefers is "small" by human standards, maybe it is the naked faith of St. John of the Cross or the childlike journey of Thérèse de Lisieux (which was the exact opposite of infantility, as we have noted). And who knows, maybe the God who accepted Job's harsh reproaches or Jacob's blows in that nocturnal tussle might have gotten a certain enjoyment out of the dispute that Nietzsche and many others engaged in with Him? Maybe He even accepted what was hidden somewhere in that apparently blasphemous, but in fact utterly sincere and painful, outcry of the man who vainly sought Him in that night of grief after the death of his granddaughter.

What Jesus had to say about the last judgment assures us that God will accept *implicit, anonymous* faith, displayed in *acts of mercy*, in service to the suffering and needy, the faith of those, who, as James the apostle tells us, *will demonstrate their faith in their works* (James 2:18). It is clear from Jesus's description that the justified will also include those who do not perform those acts specifically on His account, who have no "pious" motive at all—they simply do it on account of the suffering people themselves. They don't recognize Jesus in them and maybe they haven't even heard of Him, or they have never heard about Him in a manner whereby they might explicitly join the visible family of those who worship Him. That's why they will ask in *amazement*: "Lord, when did we see you?" And Christ, who never ceases to amaze, will amaze them—and then, with the opposite outcome, He will amaze with His answer to the selfsame question from those who never stop invoking His name but fail to see Him in the suffering and needy.[4]

Do there exist other forms of "implicit" or "anonymous" faith, which might also have hopes of ensuring a place at the right hand of Christ to those who live it? Isn't He who conceals great things in small things and shows His strength in the weak also present somehow in the faith of those in whom it consists solely of seeking, of an unsated hunger for the truth and meaning, and of unremitting questions? Isn't it in the faith of the Zacchaeuses, who are still concealed in their hiding places and peeping out very unobtrusively? And in the faith that simply takes the form of unarticulated longing? And in the faith in which there is more trembling than firmness, more questions than answers, more doubts than certainties? And also in the faith that is already weary with its endless traveling—when the goal is still nowhere in sight?

And if we were to bargain with the Lord like Abraham over Sodom[5]—would we not find a certain kind of "implicit, anonymous faith" in a number of women and men who engage sincerely in passionate disputes with God, the churches, and religion, a faith that—to their amazement—will be acceptable in God's eyes? What if at least ten of them will be found there?

৵

In the closing crescendo of his paean to love, St. Paul writes that love is patient.[6] Yes, and faith too is patient, if it really is faith. Faith *is* patience, in fact. In the same way that love for another person—its strength and authenticity—manifests and proves itself in its patience with the other, so also is *faith* present (albeit hidden, implicit, and anonymous) in a certain form of patience in the face of all of life's difficulties, hardships, and ambiguities. And it is in that patience—and maybe above all therein—that its strength and authenticity manifest themselves.

Yes, maybe the authenticity of faith demonstrates itself more through its patience than through its conscious "content"—i.e., how and what it is capable of saying precisely about its "subject." "Patience obtains everything" was the belief and teaching of St. Teresa of Avila, another great and wise doctor of the church. "By your perseverance you will secure your lives," says scripture. Nowadays faith is very much stressed as a decision, a conscious decision to follow Christ—sometimes taken in the emotional atmosphere of "charismatic" rallies. However, it requires not just a decision, but also perseverance and patience in what will come afterward.

If patience is what gives faith its strength, can it be just a marginal aspect of it? Isn't patience precisely that opening through which *God's grace* is poured into our faith, the very first cause of our salvation—and isn't that grace in fact the patience of His love for us, the patience of His trust in us? Isn't the patience of human faith the hearth in which God can light the fire of His Spirit and recast "human faith" as *the faith of God*—albeit very small, and scarcely visible in the world's eyes, but capable of performing miracles?

Or is it more accurate to say that He was always hidden, even in those *most human* forms of our seeking, inquiring, and watching—so long as it was done with *patience*, and in fact He covertly offered us that *grace of patience* that will eventually enable us to discover and recognize the Hidden One and hear Him when He calls us by name?

In the final analysis, the patience we exercise in the face of life's constant enigmas, by resisting the temptation to defect and resort to simplistic answers, is always *our patience with God,* who is not "at hand." But what else is faith but this openness in the face of God's hiddenness, the bold "yes" (or at least yearnful "maybe") of our hope in the profound stillness of God's silence, that small but tenacious flame that bursts forth again and again from the ashes of resignation even in the longest, darkest, and coldest of nights? In Christianity there is no way of separating faith and hope—and patience is their common attribute and fruit.

If God exercises such patience with us, can we refuse him our own patience of faith, hope, and love, with all the limitations of our human frailty—even at moments when we don't receive all the certainty and comfort we would maybe wish, at moments of darkness and emptiness, when there is no alternative but to wait or defect from the path of waiting?

Even the mysterious and paradoxical world of faith is formed in such a way that what often seems to be peripheral when viewed from outside turns out, once we are inside, to be surprisingly close to the center. The temple of faith can also conceal dark and empty places even in its most sacred parts, in the same way that there was a dark and empty "holy of holies" at the heart of the Temple of Jerusalem—and it was precisely there, *within it,* that God and His glory dwelled most fully.

"Waiting on God" does not happen only in the "anteroom of faith" but belongs also at the very heart of faith.

Simone Weil—who, as has already been pointed out, was, to the very end, one of those who "merely" watch and wait—penned one charming and very witty saying: "One of the most exquisite pleasures of human love—to serve the loved one without his knowing it—is only possible, as regards the love of God, through atheism."[7]

On my first cursory reading of that saying, I took it to refer to "anonymous Christians" and their "implicit" love of God; but I soon realized that it was speaking of the love of God Himself—which requires intimacy and discretion and likes to surprise us by concealing itself in anonymity. Simone leaves us uncertain as to whether she has in mind God's love, which God shows (anonymously) to atheists—and God also derives enjoyment from the fact that they overlooked Him and that He will surprise them at the very end of their journey—or whether she has in mind the grace that God shows the world covertly through atheists, hidden in a form in which we would not seek Him.

Or maybe they apply both together: God is hidden within atheists both to them and to the world, so that at the end of the ages He will bring to end this game of hide-and-seek and allow the atheists to enjoy discovering that He has been present in their lives, that they have done good through Him and through His (hidden) power—and the world (including Christians) will be surprised and gratified to discover that what atheists sometimes surprised them with was actually a gift and a "coded message" from God, that it was His mysterious presence within them.

Yes, to believe in a God we can't see also means, at the very least, to hope that He is where we can't see Him and often where we are absolutely convinced that He is not and could not be.

One evening, after extremely lengthy and very tiring discussions with one young man, who, like me, was unable for years to make up his mind whether he believed in God or not—and if he believed in Him, whether he believed in Him sufficiently—I told him: "You know, it's not so important to be sure that you believe in God. In fact, what is most important of all isn't whether *you* believe in Him. The fundamental thing is that *God believes in you*. And maybe at this particular moment it is enough for you to be aware of that."

Even though I didn't quote any of the classics, I'm sure that it was a sentence that I had used in confessionals plenty of times before, although I'm not sure whether it brought those previous persistent seekers, who were often still too inward-looking and focused on *their own* seeking, the same sense of relief it did that young man then. Faith is not something we do, faith is reliance; in our faith we ought not to take ourselves too seriously, or the degree of our knowledge and forms of *our* conviction; instead, we ought to take God very seriously. Even in religious seeking it is possible for people to go fatefully astray if they are so absorbed with *their own* seeking that they ignore the crucial fact that God is already seeking them.

The encounter at the heart of faith is possible because *God believes in us,* that He believes in us with His divine—i.e., passionate yet patient—faith. That does not mean, of course, that *He believes we exist*—in the same way that the faith He expects of us is something other and more profound than our conviction that He *exists*. Nor does it mean that He is convinced of our virtuousness and banks on our good behavior. Let us not confuse the statement that God believes in us with what parents say to their children before an examination or a school outing—"I believe in you" or "We believe in you"—because that nice-sounding expression can often imply a combination of encouragement and moral blackmail; how easily it can turn into the dreaded rebuke: "And we believed in you so much!"

God's unconditional belief and trust in us creates the scope of our freedom. God gives us freedom, even though He knows perfectly well how we treat it and will continue to treat it. Indeed, He knows and permits even the most tragic results of our treatment of His gift. He demonstrates how limitlessly and unconditionally He honors our freedom. In fact, the very *possibility* of damnation is no more, in the final analysis, than the consistent expression of God's respect for our freedom, and should this dreadful possibility become reality for some human being (something, happily, we cannot be sure of about anyone), then it would indicate that God's respect for our freedom is even greater than His infinite mercy.

I previously quoted the words of Meister Eckhart, that "the eye that we see God with is the eye that God sees us with." Could this saying also be applied by analogy to belief, so that we might say the faith with which we believe in God is the faith whereby God believes in us?

No, I'm not trying to say categorically that God's belief in us is limited by the capacity of our faith and that His belief is thus contingent (and thus also very small, we would have to add!). That would be sheer blasphemy. The *small faith* that was discussed a moment ago was, on the contrary, "the faith of God," and it was *small* only from the point of view of our world.

We also read about love—which is, after all, the sister of faith—that God loved us before we loved Him, that He loved us "while we were still sinners,"[8] that He—and His love, because He is love—

"is greater than our hearts."[9] Just as His love precedes ours and bears all the capacity of our love, so—I believe—does His faith precede ours and bear our faith, enabling it and being present within it. God Himself is present in our faith: traditional theology expresses this truth with the words "faith is grace."

But precisely on account of that mysterious presence I am convinced that our faith is more than we can see, experience, or imagine. If He is present in our faith, He is often hidden there, or simply transcendent—transcending what we infer about our faith, what we "see" in it, how we understand it (not to mention what we infer about the faith of others!). If our faith contains Him, who is greater than anything we can imagine, and if our human faith is "greater" than we realize, then the great God can be concealed *somehow* even in our apparently *small* (in the eyes of others and sometimes of ourselves) faith, as well as in our seeking and struggles. After all, haven't we plenty of evidence that God loves paradoxes?

ॐ

One of the great seekers, the Prague-born Franz Kafka, left behind him an oeuvre full of riddles and paradoxes. I have returned to his books again and again since my high-school years, and each time I discover something new. I have long since stopped asking the question "What did the author have in mind?" The books exist independently of the author's intention, and they are open to all interpretations and mental associations that they progressively evoke in us, as we live through new historical experiences and new phases of our own life stories, our own *trials,* our own waiting outside the closed gates of the castle.

Are *The Trial* and *The Castle* parables about the fate of human-kind, lost and gripped with trepidation at the incomprehensibility of the alienated machinery of modern bureaucratic society—or are they something of much profounder significance? Are they an expression of human despair in the face of God's inaccessible silence, hemmed in by the impenetrable walls and locked doors of the Law—doors that the apostle Paul tried to break through when he declared that we approach the throne of grace not through the Law but through faith, and Nietzsche tried to breach by his belief that the God of the Law was dead and we were free? Is it not an account of how Josef K.—i.e., *anyone*—is guilty, guilty of leading an empty life on the surface of the days, without love and responsibility, of how he wasted the opportunity to recognize his guilt (and it is no excuse that the Fair Trial was enciphered in absurdities and petty sordidness as in a confused and feverish nightmare)? Does this picture of *The Trial* and *The Castle* reflect cabalistic teaching about how human beings are constantly judged and how the initial stages of the heavenly judgment already take place on earth and are interwoven indiscernibly into our everyday lives? Was it a clear-sighted prophecy about the absurd trials that the innocent would soon be subjected to in the horrifyingly relentless machinery of Nazism and Communism? Or in some way do all these possible interpretations apply and Kafka's works are trying to tell us something that is hard to accept—something as repellent as the words of the Old Testament prophets when they said that God's hand was behind the catastrophes that befell God's people—namely, that what paved the way for the gruesome nightmares of the twentieth century was precisely the rootless, superficial, and feckless life of the semi-anonymous modern *Anyone*?

In the novel *The Trial,* one of the most important books of the twentieth century, one frequently encounters episodes that are clearly crucial to understanding the message of the entire work. Might they not inspire some of our meditations on the theme of Zacchaeus?

Kafka places the following parable in the mouth of a priest who has, surprisingly, addressed Josef K. *by name* in the cathedral, where K. was seeking someone else entirely.

> *There is a man sitting in front of the gateway to the Law, who has tried for years to enter but has found no way to. The gateway is guarded by a powerful gatekeeper, who indicates that after him come other gatekeepers who are even more powerful and obdurate than he is. At the moment the life of the "man from the country" is fading and his waiting is coming to its end, he begs the doorkeeper with his last remaining strength to answer one single question: Why, over all these years, given that everyone wants access to the Law, has no one but me asked to be let in? And the doorkeeper replies to the dying man: Because this gateway was intended for you alone. Now I'll go and close it.*

Let us return to our third apocrypha—Zacchaeus the penitent.

Let us imagine that Zacchaeus *too* is already dead tired from his wandering and vain waiting. He has again missed Rosh Hashanah, and Yom Kippur is approaching once more. During the days of repentance, Zacchaeus is preparing to return his life to the Lord and with it his unfulfilled task. But he is troubled by the question of why he didn't succeed. He wonders what he might have overlooked or failed to hear. Where did he go wrong? And at that moment—on the very eve of the Day of Atonement—a voice suddenly arises from his heart—but not the same as the one that always held him back each time he was ready to announce the fulfillment of his mission. This time it really is the voice of Christ, which cannot be missed.

"Zacchaeus," says the Lord, "your name means 'pure'—and this time it became a trap in this stage of your journey. You yourself made the task tougher than the one you'd been given—like that time when you promised to make a greater recompense than justice required and more than you were capable of making. And this time too your willful decision to make the requirements stricter was not out of generous love, but instead you fell for the temptation of the one who always falsifies God's commandments and makes them more restrictive, the one who tried to persuade Adam and Eve that God had forbidden them to eat from *any* of the trees in the Garden of Eden, as a means of provoking the wish to eat from the *only tree* that was forbidden. You yourself insisted that you had to hear my voice in its absolute *purity*, with no human weaknesses, doubts, and searching mixed in. But my voice has never been heard in that way in human history since the day I ascended into heaven. My words, my legacy, and my name are entrusted to the lips of people who are never completely pure, to hearts in which love for me is always mixed with love for the self and for the things of this world. I gave myself to the faith of my church, which is made up of sinners, not angels, and I was also in those who are still far from its visible gates, those who are grimy and sweaty from their seeking and wandering along paths full of questions and doubts. They are the ones you should have listened to above all; it was in them above all that you should have sought me.

"And there's another thing. Faith—if it's a living faith—has to breathe; it has its days and its nights. God speaks not only through His words but also through His silence. He speaks to people not only through His closeness, but also through His remoteness. You forgot to listen for my voice in those experiencing my silence, my remoteness, those who gaze from the other side, from the vale of darkness, at the mountain of my mystery, hidden in a cloud. That's where you should have sought me. They're the ones you should have come with, whom you should have brought a little closer to my threshold. That was the gate prepared *especially for you*."

And Zacchaeus falls on his face and weeps. And Zacchaeus the tax collector says: "Lord, what confused me on my journey was also the pride I never wanted to admit. I always made great demands on myself, but I was never able to live up to them. And because I wasn't able to admit it, I would make exaggerated demands on others. I didn't hear Your voice in them because I scorned their imperfections, their *impurity*. And though I was unable to admit it, in doing so I was judging them and lording it over them. I was more or less saying: 'Thank you, Lord, that I, Zacchaeus the tax collector, am not like the rest, that I am not like that Pharisee.' Forgive me, Lord."

And because Zacchaeus is, after all, a son of Abraham, who has been found once again, the Lord says to him, "Come down from the tree of your pride, Zacchaeus. Today, for a change, you must dine with me in *my* house. And remember: you must never again narrow the gate to my house. You can only enter my house in the company of others; it is not a gate for you alone. *Now I'll go and open it.*"

Written in the hermitage of a contemplative monastery in the Rhineland in July and August 2007.

Notes

INTRODUCTION

1. In an exactly symmetrical vein—and legitimately—the postmodern philosopher Slavoj Žižek writes: "the authentic Christian legacy is much too precious to be left to the fundamentalist freaks." *The Fragile Absolute: Or, Why Is the Christian Legacy Worth Fighting For?* (London, New York, 2001), Verso 2001, p. 2.
2. Cf. 2 Cor. 12:7–10.

1. ADDRESSING ZACCHAEUS

1. In other translations, a mulberry tree.
2. Cf. Matt. 22:11–14

2. BLESSED ARE THE DISTANT

1. Cf. Eph. 4:18; Luke 11:44; Mark 6:34; Luke 9:58, etc.
2. Cf. Matt. 25:31–46
3. Garry Wills, *What Jesus Meant* (New York: Viking, 2006), pp. 66–75
4. There have been very interesting results from extensive psychological research of a classic of Nordic psychology of religion, Hjalmar Sundén, concerning the success of different types of believing parents in passing on their faith to their children. Least successful were those who were "too certain," because they turned their children off with their authoritarianism, as well as those who were "too uncertain," because their

faith was too vague and unconvincing. The most successful were those who were "slightly uncertain," who were also capable of tolerating critical questions and doubts and tended to educate by personal example. Cf. Nils G. Holm, *Scandinavian Psychology of Religion* (Abo Akademi: Finland, 1987).

5. The lecture was given in Mannheim, Germany, in April 2004. Cf. Tomáš Halík, *Vzýván i nevzýván* (Prague: Nakladatelství Lidové noviny), pp. 131–45.

6. James H. Forest, *Living with Wisdom: A Life of Thomas Merton* (New York: Orbis Books, 1991).

3. FAR FROM ALL SUNS

1. Cf. Friedrich Nietzsche, *The Gay Science,* ed. Walter Kaufmann (New York: Vintage, 1974), pp. 181–82.

2. Jean-François Six, *Vie de Thérèse de Lisieux* (Paris: Seuil, 1975).

3. This is also mentioned by Jean-François Six in the cited biography of St. Thérèse in the context of the church of her day.

4. T. R. Nevin, *Therese of Lisieux, God's Gentle Warrior* (New York: Oxford Press, 2006).

5. Nonetheless, in his brief essay on the occasion of the centenary of Thérèse de Lisieux, Karl Rahner, one of the greatest twentieth-century theologians, considered that what was most important and remarkable was that the church had recognized this strange death in darkness as a "holy death," not only through her official canonization, but also through a century of fervent veneration. Cf. Karl Rahner, "Tod als Aufgang des Lichts." In: *Im Herzen der Kirche: Therese von Lisieux und ihre Sendung* (Mariazell: Verlag Christliche Innerlichkeit, 1973), pp. 34–36.

6. Cf. 1 Cor. 13:4 and subs.

7. Cf. 1 Cor. 13:8.

8. Hans Urs von Balthasar, *Therese of Lisieux,* trans. Donald Nicholl (New York: Sheed and Ward, 1954).

9. Ibid.

10. Cf. Rev. 21:22.

11. Phil. 2:6–11.

12. Cf. Gianni Vattimo, *After Christianity*, trans. Luca D'Isanto (New York: Columbia University Press, 2002).

13. Gilbert K. Chesterton, *Orthodoxy* (New York: Dodd, Mead & Co., 1908).

4. BAREFOOT

1. It was at the World Missionary Congress in Paris on August 25, 2006; I will come back to these thoughts in chapter 7 of the present book.

2. Cf. Joseph Moingt, "Laisser Dieu s'en aller," in *Dieu, Église, Société* (Paris: Centurion, 1985).

3. Cf. Rom. 8:26.

4. "*Gaudium et Spes:* The Pastoral Constitution on the Church in the Modern World," December 7, 1965.

5. Cf. Luke 14:33.

6. Some Christians understood and accepted the years of Communist persecution as an "exodus," as a distressful but also meaningful and purifying journey from the stage of material security in bourgeois society; it came as a painful surprise for many that after the fall of Communism, no "promised land" awaited the church and society, but instead another demanding journey, demanding in a different way.

7. This question, inspired by a text by Jan Ámos Komenský (Comenius), a seventeenth-century bishop of the persecuted Unitas Fratrum, was raised during the period of Communism in Czechoslovakia by one of my teachers, Oto Mádr. Father Mádr's brief text "Modus moriendi církve" (in: Oto Mádr, Jolana Poláková, *Slovo o této době* [Prague: Zvon, 1992]) may be regarded as one of the few attempts at a specific theology of liberation for the countries under Communist rule.

8. In the Czech lands, a poignant example of that kind was the leading nineteenth-century writer and journalist Karel Havlíček Borovský, the founder of modern Czech political thought (whose statue now stands in Chicago by Lake Michigan).

9. Cf. Exodus 3:5.

5. THE DISPUTE ABOUT THE BEAUTY OF DULCINEA DEL TOBOSO

1. Ronald Rolheiser, *The Holy Longing: The Search for a Christian Spirituality* (New York: Doubleday, 1999), p. 137.

2. Cf. Charles J. Sykes, *A Nation of Victims: The Decay of the American Character* (New York: St. Martin's Press, 1993).

3. Cf. 1 Cor. 12:12–21.

4. Letter sent by Gertrud von Le Fort to H. von Schubert in 1926, quoted from M. von Schwarzkopf and Gertrud von Le Fort in B. Moser, *Grosse Gestalten des Glaubens* (Munich: Sudwest Verlag, 1982), p. 490.

5. Cf. Luke 15:11–32.

6. Cf. 1 Cor. 13:12.

7. John Paul II and many others rightly pointed out that the inhabitants of the Communist-ruled countries had never ceased to feel and never stopped being Europeans, even within the Soviet empire, and that European integration and the admission of new countries to the European Union is not a "broadening of Europe" but rather the "Europeanization of the European Union."

8. On November 8, 1620, the Catholic forces of Maximilian I, duke of Bavaria, commanded by Count von Tilly, defeated the Protestant forces of Bohemia at White Mountain (Bílá Hora) near Prague. There followed the re-Catholicization of the Bohemian kingdom.

6. A LETTER

1. Cf. Phil. 2:7–8.

2. Cf. Isa. 53:3–4.

3. A similar interpretation, with many more references to the context of Nietzsche's life and work, is to be found in Richard Elliott Friedman, *The Disappearance of God: A Divine Mystery* (Boston: Little, Brown, 1995).

4. Cf., for instance, Paul C. Vitz, *Sigmund Freud's Christian Unconscious* (New York: Guilford Press, 1988).

5. Nietzsche demonstrated that our very rationality, our science, our logic, and the very structure of our language are still the "shadow of the dead God"—they still, yet under other names, operate within the theologi-

cal and metaphysical concept of Truth, which we ourselves did not create and go on "not creating." Many forms of "atheism" simply changed
the name of God and His order, but they did not get rid of Him.

7. UNKNOWN YET TOO CLOSE

1. Cf. Matt. 12:45.
2. Peter Hünermann, "Der fremde Gott—Verheissung für das europäische
Haus," in Michael J. Buckley, Peter Hünermann, *Gott—ein Fremder in un-
serem Haus?: Die Zukunft des Glaubens in Europa* (Freiburg: Herder, 1996),
p. 204. The same author, in a commentary on a European value orientation study that found that 4 percent of Europeans describe themselves as
atheists, but only 35 percent believe in a "living God" (18 percent don't
know, and 35 percent believe in a "higher power"), noted, "For two
thirds of Europe's inhabitants God is an alien God." Peter Hünermann,
"Der fremde Gott: Eine theologische Reflexion," in Stephan Pauly
(Hsg.), *Der fremde Gott in unserer Zeit* (Stuttgart: Kuhlhammer, 1998).
3. Cf. Tomáš Halík, *Vzýván i nevzýván* (Prague: Nakladatelství Lidové
noviny, 2004), pp. 321–38.
4. Cf. Acts 17:19–18:1.
5. Cf. Luther's Great Catechism.
6. Stay a while, thou art so beautiful.

8. THE EASTER MIRROR

1. Cf. Gal. 5:1.
2. Alain Badiou, *Saint Paul: The Foundation of Universalism,* trans. Ray
Brassier (Stanford, CA: Stanford University Press, 2003).
3. Friedrich Nietzsche, *The Antichrist,* trans. H. L. Mencken (New York:
Knopf, 1918), p. 42.
4. Of course it is not my intention to deny the mystical and philosophical
dimensions of the Judaic and Islamic traditions, but I cannot find any radically antilegalistic thinker like Paul at the very heart of those traditions.
5. Cf. Isa. 55:8–9.
6. Cf. 1 Cor. 2:2.

7. More about this in Tomáš Halík, *Confessor's Night* (New York: Double-day Religion, 2010).

8. Cf. Rom. 6:4.

9. Cf. 1 Cor. 1:18–25.

10. Cf. Matt. 28:12–15.

9. A TIME TO GATHER STONES

1. Cf. Eccles. 3:1–8.

2. I described my experiences from those trips around the six continents—including my participation in an expedition to the Antarctic—an experiment in survival in conditions of extreme psychological and physical pressure—in my book *Co je bez chvění, není pevné* [What doesn't quiver isn't firm] (Prague: Lidové noviny, 2002).

3. Cf. Isa. 52:7.

4. Cf. Garry Wills, *What Jesus Meant* (New York: Viking, 2006), p. 2.

5. Cf. Matt. 26:52.

6. Cf. John 18:36.

7. Cf. Matt. 10:36.

8. Cf. Luke 17:1.

9. Cf. Tomáš Halík, *Vzýván i nevzýván* (Prague: Nakladatelství Lidové noviny, 2004), pp. 38–40.

10. Cf. J. Sacks, "Sedra Toldot" and "Sedra Vayishlach," in his Torah commentary: *Covenant and Conversation*. Available at http://www.chiefrabbi.org/thoughts/index.html.

10. A TIME TO HEAL

1. Cf. Mark 9:5.

2. Cf. John 20:19–23.

3. Cf. Gen. 2:7.

4. Cf. Ps. 104:29.

5. Cf. Ps. 104:30.

6. Cf. Rev. 2:17.

7. Genesis 3:10.

8. Mark 5:27–34.

9. Drewermann, E., *Wort des Heils—Wort der Heilung* (Düsseldorf 1990), pp. 87–92.

10. Matt. 7:29.

11. Matt. 16:13–20.

12. John 14:9.

13. News is now emerging from South Africa with increasing frequency in the year in which I am writing this book that in spite of efforts made by the celebrated "Truth and Reconciliation Commission" (inspired by Archbishop Desmond Tutu), many conflicts remain unresolved and "wounds of the past" are still open and unhealed.

14. Cf. Matt. 11:30.

11. ST. ZACCHAEUS

1. R. E. Friedman, *The Disappearance of God* (Boston: Little, Brown, 1995), pp. 188–92.

2. Cf. Ezek. 12:1–12.

3. Cf. Ezek. 24:1–14.

4. Cf. Ezek. 37:15–28.

5. Cf. Simone Weil, *Seventy Letters,* trans. Robert Rees (London: Oxford University Press, 1965).

12. ETERNAL ZACCHAEUS

1. Tomáš Halík, *Noc zpovědníka* (Prague 2005), 28–34.

2. Cf. Luke 17:5–7.

3. Cf. 1 Cor. 1:25–28.

4. Cf. Matt. 25:31–46.

5. Cf. Gen. 18:20–32.

6. 1 Cor. 13:4.

7. Simone Weil, *First and Last Notebooks,* trans. Richard Rees (London, New York: Oxford University Press, 1970), p. 84.

8. Cf. Rom. 5:8.

9. Cf. 1 John 3:20.